Indian
Inspirations

by Gisela Thwaites

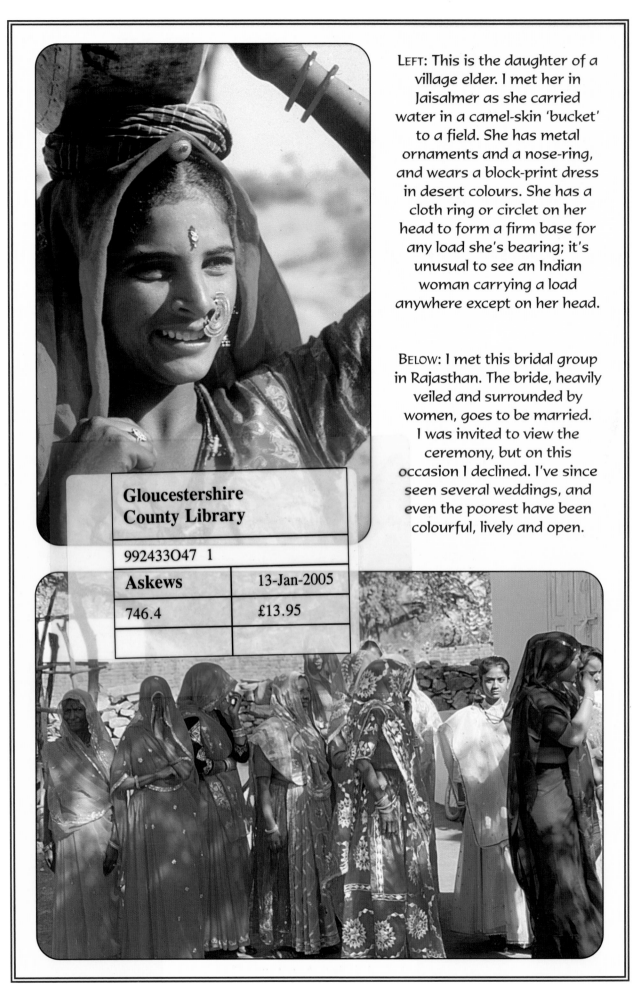

LEFT: This is the daughter of a village elder. I met her in Jaisalmer as she carried water in a camel-skin 'bucket' to a field. She has metal ornaments and a nose-ring, and wears a block-print dress in desert colours. She has a cloth ring or circlet on her head to form a firm base for any load she's bearing; it's unusual to see an Indian woman carrying a load anywhere except on her head.

BELOW: I met this bridal group in Rajasthan. The bride, heavily veiled and surrounded by women, goes to be married. I was invited to view the ceremony, but on this occasion I declined. I've since seen several weddings, and even the poorest have been colourful, lively and open.

Indian Inspirations

A feast of patchwork, embroidery and beadwork techniques and projects

Gisela Thwaites

TRAPLET

PUBLICATIONS

Craftworld Series

ABOUT THE AUTHOR

GISELA THWAITES is an established hand quilter, and was for many years a tutor at the Liberty Sewing School in London. Over the last few years she has developed a fresh approach to patchwork and quilting, characterised by embellishment and the bold juxtaposition of colours and fabrics. This new direction developed from – and is reinforced by – her annual visits to India and her study of Indian textiles and embroidery techniques.

Drawing on her experience as a needlewoman, Gisela offers this book as a resource for crazy patchwork enthusiasts of all skill levels. In the book she introduces many simple Indian-style embroidery stitches and techniques, then shows numerous ways in which you can use them to enhance your own patchwork and quilting, including a wide range of stitched and beaded projects.

Gisela has contributed to a number of books and specialist needlework publications, and she exhibits, demonstrates and teaches widely.

For Ilona and Emma

PLEASE NOTE:

*Measurements in the book are given in both imperial and metric;
for best results when you're following the project instructions,
work in one system or the other without mixing them.*

First published in 2003 by
Traplet Publications Limited
Traplet House, Severn Drive, Upton upon Severn,
Worcestershire WR8 0JL

Publisher: Tony Stephenson

Text and designs © Gisela Thwaites

All illustrations by Gail Lawther, © Traplet Publications
Studio scans and pre-press work by Neil Blowers

ISBN 1 900371 61 8
British Library Cataloguing in Publication Data
A catalogue record for this book is available from the British Library

Designed and edited by Teamwork,
Christopher & Gail Lawther, 44 Rectory Walk,
Sompting, Lancing, West Sussex BN15 0DU

Set in Usherwood, Stone Sans and Formal Script

Printed by Wa Fai Graphic Arts Printing Co., Hong Kong

CONTENTS

Why India?

India is different. Anyone visiting India and arriving at a major airport in Delhi or Mumbai is struck by the noise, the throngs of people, the colours, the sheer energy and the 'foreign-ness' of it all. It could be nowhere but India. The dress is mixed: western clothes mingle with saris, Nehru frocks and kurtas, and a few dhotis. And the headwear is almost as varied, from turbans to caps – some richly ornamented. The buildings in the major cities include western hotels (recognisably cosmopolitan even with their touches of India), concrete and brick skyscrapers, and old-style multi-storey native dwellings. And on the edges of the cities, great areas of shanty town, featuring mud roads, tin roofs, hessian and tin walls – and lived in by the poorest people. And everywhere, beggars.

In the cities you can find shops and stores equivalent to those in any major European town and, in contrast, narrow roads full of vegetable stalls, silversmiths, and shops selling household goods. Open markets and bazaars exist in every quarter. Roads are busy: buses with passengers clinging to the outside, expensive cars, bicycle rickshaws (and rickshaws pulled by men, often bare-footed), oxen hauling carts, and vast, noisy lorries, highly decorated and packed with people and goods. Small three-wheeled 'taxis' (phut-phuts), looking like motorised hansom cabs, criss-cross the roads in competition with cyclists and walkers. The abiding impression is of almost overwhelming vitality.

Provincial towns and villages, lacking the larger, western-style shops, are as full of activity and energy as the big cities. Workshops, vegetable markets, shops selling fabrics, sweet shops, hardware stores, cobblers, barbers and food stalls are everywhere. And everywhere you find

Woman-power! A common sight: a woman carrying firewood, crops or – in this case – animal fodder from the fields to the village.

lots and lots of people, often colourfully dressed, all doing something or going somewhere. The smallest villages share the same characteristics, of colour, business, variety and noise – voices, vehicles, hooters and sirens.

Animals too are ubiquitous: camels, oxen, ponies, goats and cows. The smallest villages have electricity, although power cuts and supply failures are common, and you can find temples and schools wherever you go.

ABOVE: On my first visit to India I went to the Suraj Kund Mela, outside Delhi; the Mela is a giant government-sponsored craft fair, and each state in turn sets the theme. When I went, it was the turn of Orissa, famous for its colourful appliqué work such as the parasols and lanterns you can see here. The vivid colours, mirror-work and craftsmanship 'turned me on'! The turbanned men, by the way, form a band – you can see their drums behind them.

RIGHT: The Mela I visited offered entertainment, too. Here you can see a family of dancers: father is on the hobby-horse, and his two sons are performing. In the background are craft stalls and fabric displays. The huts are thatched with palm leaves and fronds.

It's not surprising that a country of such vigour and contrast also presents the eye of the visitor with a wide variety of fabrics, textiles, dress and styles. There are of course regional variations, but the lasting and overall impression is of colour, varied material and rich ornamentation. Dress is highly decorated and vividly coloured. The ornamentation includes mirrors, beads, and gold and silver metallic threads, woven into fabrics or used to embroider patterns, many of which are highly intricate.

The embroidery uses many of the stitches familiar to us in the west: herringbone, open chain stitch, chain stitch and blanket stitch (see pages 23-27) and, for both embroidery and quilting, darning stitch. The simplicity of the stitches encourages the most inexperienced of needle-workers and quilters to embroider and then to enrich and embellish their work. Although you won't hear the village craftswoman talk of crewel needles or appliqué needles, she does use a range of needles immediately recognisable to any quilter or embroiderer. Inevitably there are some minor differences in the way the Indian stitcher approaches embroidery; for instance, the ari hook, used by cobblers to sew shoes and sandals together, is widely used for creating chain stitch, and the vast majority of Indian craftspeople sit cross-legged on the ground to do their work.

It's not easy to buy beads and mirrors in the towns and cities – certainly not in shops. You need to go through the bazaars to buy these and other sewing materials, and in the bazaars everything is sold by weight: wool, metal, beads, gold and silver, mirrors etc are dispensed by the ounce. Embroidery designs, in the villages particularly, are what we'd describe as primitive or naive, often using animals (camels, elephants, horses and donkeys), or their gods, as motifs. Much of the embroidery, and all Kashmiri embroidery, is worked in chain stitch, but other forms of ornamentation show regional differences; the Gujarati and Rajasthani methods of fixing mirrors to dresses and hangings, for

ABOVE: Old and new! An ox pulls a mowing machine near Humayan's tomb in Old Delhi.

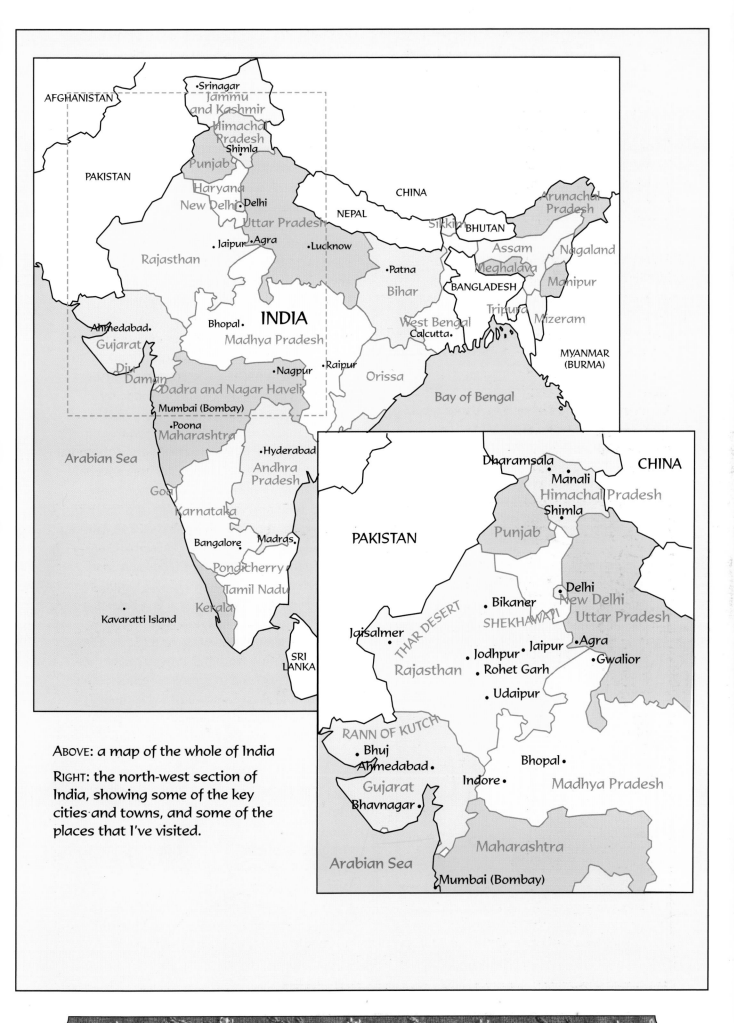

ABOVE: a map of the whole of India

RIGHT: the north-west section of India, showing some of the key cities and towns, and some of the places that I've visited.

I took this photograph in Ahmedabad in a refuge which I support for battered women and children. It's run as a co-operative, and here you see an older woman tutoring a young girl in design. A little later they were working the treadle sewing machine in the background.

We had to stop while this man sniffed opium in the middle of a hillside road. It's not uncommon.

example, are quite different (see pages 29-30), and it's easy to distinguish between the dress and ornamentation of different areas.

The main cotton mills of northern and northwestern India are in Gujarat (although Madras is noted for its checked cottons) and the fabrics generally have a looser weave than we're used to in the west. The Indian silks (dupion, metallic silk tissue and brocade) are good to work with, and I particularly love the brocade of metallic threads shot with silk. Many fabrics are dyed locally, using vegetable and mineral dyes, and even in remote villages they can be seen hanging out to dry outside the houses.

Tie-dyeing and block printing are now seen in many parts of the world, but until quite recently were particularly characteristic of India. You can see blocks being made by roadside wood-workers or (as I did) in the Tibetan markets; these are now common in the northern states, following the flight of the Dalai Lama from Tibet when the Chinese moved in. In one Tibetan monastery workshop I saw elderly men and women using just a few tools to carve the most complex shapes and intricate designs in jacaranda wood. These blocks, varying in size from a few inches across to rectangles about 12 inches by 20, would later be on sale in the bazaars for a few rupees.

In the Saurashtra area of Gujarat I sat with a woman learning from her how to make the beaded covers used to upholster chairs, tables and cupboards (see page 40). These heavy 'cloths' of beads are used also for personal wear, and are attractive and serviceable. The woman, sitting cross-legged on the ground, had no scissors, and bit the ends off the threads as necessary. Pretty primitive, but very effective! And this, for me, is so typical of the India I know: rudimentary tools, poor working conditions, but the most exciting and attractive materials and embellishments.

It's the wonderful country of India, and its textiles and crafts, which inspired me to write this book so that I can introduce you to the same colourful world.

ABOVE: I spent several hours with block-makers and block-printers at Bagro, Jaipur. The block-maker squats at a three-legged workbench and chips designs with fine metal chisels and gouges. But note the hammer – and the bare feet. I brought a few of these blocks home with me.

The groom from the Rajasthani wedding (see page 2); led by his mother, he's processing towards the wedding ceremony. The marigold garland is traditional. Many houses, like this one, have murals on their outside walls.

Materials and Equipment

MATERIALS

Fabrics

Personal taste obviously is one of the main influences on your choice of fabrics, but texture, weave, weight and appearance will all play their part in helping you to decide which fabric to use for a particular purpose. I use a wide variety of fabrics in my work.

I generally use American muslin (what we usually call calico in England) as a foundation fabric; on top of this foundation I mostly use speciality silk fabrics such as dupion, silk ikat, silk tissue, silk organza, and silk brocade. As a quilter and embroiderer I love silk; it produces wonderful effects, and can make the simplest piece of stitching look truly special.

I use also some undyed silks: these are intended for printing and dyeing, but should be washed first. This group includes silk mousseline, silk organza, habotai, silk noil and the lovely tussah silks. It's also possible to buy silk velvet, and a mixture of silk and cotton. This latter is a 57% silk and 43% cotton mix which is a very useful fabric with a lovely sheen; it has the strength of cotton and the beauty of silk. It's suitable for most needlework, and takes dyes beautifully.

These fabrics are mainly plain – that is, without designs printed on them – and that makes them ideal for embroidery and for putting your own 'stamp' on them. All of these fabrics are available from The Silk Route (see page 119). And of course I do use other fabrics as well as silks. These include lace, brocade, hand-marbled fabrics, crunches (fabrics which have been scrunched up in water – see below!), tie-dyes, batik and some of the lovely Hoffman range. Whatever fabric you choose – silk or cotton – it's up to you to bring out the best in the material and the embroidery.

TOP: I watched these colourful brocades being made by disabled men in a cramped workshop in Mansa. The spooled yarn is wound onto a shuttle, which is then thrown across the weaving frame; the warp is tie-dyed, the weft is plain. The whole process is done by hand.

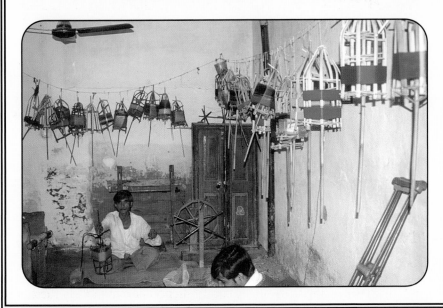

BELOW: Here you can see the workshop, containing a spinning wheel, spools of yarn and – at the rear – the shuttles. Note the crutches leaning against the wall, and the electric ceiling fan. The weaving frame is in the adjoining room.

Pros and cons

Now let's look more closely at the merits and drawbacks of some of the fabrics I use most.

• For me, **American muslin** is the ideal foundation fabric: its fairly open weave makes it easy to work, while its neutral colour allows you to picture relatively easily how other colours and fabrics will look when they're superimposed on it.

• **Silk velvet**, with its viscose pile and silk backing, is ideal for devoré techniques as it soaks up the dye and can give a stunning effect. But it's very slippery, and tends to move if you use it as a 'patch'. I really love using this velvet, but I always mutter a few words under my breath as it **is** difficult to handle.

• **Silk tissue** is India at its best. It's woven using coloured silk in one direction and metallic thread in the other. This process gives it what's called a 'shot' effect when it's used flat – that is, it seems to be one colour when you look at it from one direction, and a totally different one when you look at it from another. Silk tissue can also be totally transformed by scrunching it up in water, which creates an unusual fabric that's ideal for special effects and is easy to cut and sew.

• Indian **silk organza**, too, comes in a range of beautiful colours, many of which are shot. It's a fine fabric which is useful as an overlay, or in any project which includes beads and stitches. It's also ideal for shadow work, pleating and ruching.

I spent almost a day in Patan, a town in Gujarat, seeing how double ikat (or patolas) is produced. Both the warp and the weft are separately tie-dyed before weaving, and over the centuries patterns of wonderful subtlety and richness have been developed. One man will produce no more than 25cm (10in) in a day, and the result is a very expensive fabric: a double ikat sari can cost as much as £3000.

Sadly, the skills seem to be dying out. The young people leave for better jobs, and the remaining craftsmen are reluctant to pass on their skills to outsiders.

Here in Rohet Garh I practised chain stitch embroidery. The boy in the centre was my teacher – he wears the white socks I gave him earlier. I used an ari or hook to work an elephant design in chain stitch; he was as proud of my efforts as I was.

I was in Jasdan, Gujarat, when I took this photograph of a princess and her son modelling court dress. The princess is wearing the clothes worn by a man at investitures and similar court functions, while her son is dressed as a page boy. The family has a wonderful collection of saris.

• Occasionally I like to use some **silk brocade** in my work. This has gold or silver woven in as a third thread, which gives a luxuriant effect and an Indian 'feel' to whatever project you're stitching. The fabric is easy to handle and cut, but you need to be careful when you're sewing it, as it's slightly thicker than some of the other fabrics and you need to take care to keep any turnings flat.

• Most of all I love to use **dupion**. It comes in an abundance of colours, but if you simply can't find the shade you want you can take a white or cream dupion and dye it to achieve the exact colour you're after. Dupion is also useful for tie-dyeing, marbling and printing, as its weave gives it a special thick-and-thin effect. Its drawback is that it frays very easily, so allow for this by taking a slightly larger seam allowance than you would usually need. An alternative is to use Fray Check, a product available in quilt and haberdashery shops. (Incidentally, if I get a badly frayed end

I usually pull the threads out completely and make tassels or embroider with them).

Embroidery threads

There are all kinds of wonderful thread on the market, and many of these can be used extremely successfully in Indian-style embroidery and embellishment.

• Let's start with the most common **stranded threads**; the best-known manufacturers of these are Anchor and DMC. These six-stranded threads come in cotton and marlitt, a 100% viscose thread. Both are in 8-metre skeins in an extensive range of colours, and both are colourfast. Stranded threads are easy to handle, and can be used for all but the more specialised embroidery techniques; you can work with different numbers of strands in the needle, depending on the size of your stitching and on whether you want fine or chunky stitching. You can also create ornate combination stitches with these threads, for example by working a herringbone stitch in one colour and then using a contrasting one for interlacing.

• Then there are the colourfast ranges of **coton perlé** from the same manufacturers. Coton perlé No 5 is the more common one, but look out for the No 8, which is really lovely to work with – it's much finer than the No 5, and more versatile. Out of Africa (see page 119) has a variegated version of perlé which comes nearest to No 8; it's a pleasure to work with, as it gives smooth, even stitches.

• *Stranded metallic hand-embroidery threads* can be used in different combinations to create just the right thickness for any design. I particularly like the ranges of golds, silvers and bronzes which both Anchor and DMC offer, and you can use the slight differences in colour (bright and subtle) between the two types to good effect. You may also find metallic threads with a fine cotton thread inside them – but these are more difficult to use. If you use a length of this thread longer than about 40cm (15in), you'll find that it uncoils and wears through.

• There are many different *heavy metallic threads* that can be couched onto fabric and they provide a wide range of textures. Japan gold and purl are used by the more experienced embroiderer, but – be warned – you have to be pretty skilled to use them. It really does take time to create a successful goldwork design.

• For that truly special piece of embroidery, try using *space-dyed silk thread*; I buy mine from Stef Francis (see page 119). These threads come in a range of thicknesses, and are particularly interesting because of the way the colour changes as your stitching progresses. Variegated threads can change the mood of your embroidery by adding another dimension.

You might find it useful to create a sample using a few different threads at a time, so that you can judge their different effects: try a superfine thread, then work the same stitch using 12-ply silk. (Always use two strands in the needle). Try the same stitch in a thread such as spun silk with flames (one of Stef Francis' threads – see above), and then in fine silk. (These last two threads are not divided into strands.) Have a look at the animal pictures on page 79; the horse features embellishment in spun silk with flames and a border in superfine thread, while the elephant is created in fine silk, and the embellishment and border are in superfine thread.

Beads and other embellishments

Beads are absolutely indispensible to anyone embroidering and embellishing crazy patchwork, and they're available in an astonishing variety of shapes and finishes. If you visit a specialist bead shop you'll be confronted by hundreds of containers, each of which holds beads of a specific size, shape, colour and texture. You can spend many happy hours just wandering round and browsing through the containers, looking out for the beads which are just right for your work. The sheer range of choice can actually be quite overwhelming, so it's sensible to think carefully about the types of beads you're after before your visit: better still, take samples of your work or your fabrics with you, so that you can see just how the beads look in position.

Colour is very important; with Indian-style work you'll often be looking for something bright and reflective, so you may well be drawn to metallic silver or gold, but sometimes you'll want more muted shades, so have a look at purples, mauves and blacks. It's good to remember that matt finishes are often 'quieter' than shiny ones. On some beads the finish is an amalgam of colours, with one particular hue appearing more dominant as the light falls on it. The texture of the bead is also important; it affects the way that the light is reflected off the surface, and can impart a sense of hardness or softness to the bead, making some sparkle and some appear more matt.

Size and shape are other critical factors. Beads can be any size from almost unbelievably small (the tiniest ones are known as seed beads), through to gigantic ones suitable for threading onto chunky necklaces, and everything in between. Obviously it's important to choose beads that are just right for your project – if they're too big they will dominate, and if they're too insignificant they'll almost disappear. Bead shapes vary almost as much as their sizes and colours: some are flat, rather like buttons; others are spherical, like pearls. Some beads are oval (flat or rounded), long or cylindrical; the cylindrical shapes are known as bugles. Still others are made to look like precious stones.

Whatever beads you choose, remember that you have to use a needle and thread with them; I talk about needles specifically for beading in the following section, but you'll find both long straw needles (these are long and bendy) and appliqué needles useful. To prepare thread for beadwork,

I studied embroidery with this Hindu lady. She wears a bead choker, a heavy metal necklace, and many bangles; the bangles show that she is married. Her dress is rather like a pinafore – it has no back, and the long head-dress is used to cover her shoulders and back. She's an embroiderer from Bhuj, a town destroyed in a recent earthquake but considered a paradise for embroiderers.

draw it through beeswax (or a proprietary preparation such as Thread Heaven). For the thread itself I generally use Nymo, or silk threads – sometimes pulled out from odds and ends of the fabric I'm working with.

TOOLS OF THE TRADE

Your sewing equipment

Your sewing equipment should be the best quality you can get. You'll use it a great deal, and it must be effective and reliable. I suppose we all have favourite items, but as far as I'm concerned a basic sewing kit must contain: pins; a tape measure and a ruler; needles for sewing, embroidery and beading; paper scissors, fabric shears and small embroidery scissors with sharp points. An embroidery hoop is handy for both embroidery and appliqué work.

You also need a good-quality lead pencil, tracing or tissue paper, dressmaker's carbon paper, graph paper and coloured pencils. Not essential, but certainly desirable (and I couldn't do without them), are a self-healing cutting mat, a safety ruler and a rotary cutter. Let's look at some of the basics in a bit more detail.

• Invest in a good pair of ***fabric scissors or shears***; the ones with fine serrated edges are especially good for silk. You might also find ***pinking shears*** useful. You need a good pair of ***embroidery scissors***: these have short blades and sharp tips, for cutting threads or trimming small pieces of fabric accurately. Their thin, pointed blades can be used to remove unwanted stitches without damaging the background fabric.

• A medium-sized ***embroidery hoop***, 18-20cm (7-8in) in diameter, is comfortable to hold and can be moved across the fabric as the embroidery is completed.

• You'll need a variety of ***needles***. Crewel needles are the best to use for embroidery; they have large eyes that make threading them easy, and they come in various sizes. Chenille needles look like crewel needles but are much larger; they can be used to take thick couched

threads through to the wrong side of the fabric. Tapestry needles are blunt-tipped and are ideal for use on evenweave fabrics.

For thicker, fancy threads use an embroidery needle with a much larger eye. For silk ribbons, a crewel needle No 8 or 7 is usually right, but to embroider with a 2mm ribbon you'll need a smaller needle. When beading, I use appliqué or short quilting needles, No 11 or 12; these are ideal for picking up beads one by one. To my mind the needle recommended for beading, which is a straw, is too long and bendy; I use a straw only if I want to couch a length of beads or bugles.

• I have a range of ***pins***, from the 3cm (1in) ones to the 5cm (2in) ones which can hold all the layers of a quilt together.

Finishing

A word on finishing your embroidered and pieced projects. Wadding/batting isn't essential for embroidered quilts. You already have three layers of material: first, your foundation; secondly, your fabric plus embroidery and possibly beads; and thirdly, your backing. But if you feel that you do need to strengthen your embroidered quilt, or give it a quilted surround, choose a synthetic or natural-fibre wadding/batting about 2 or 2½oz in weight. For something really special, use silk wadding – which is what I used for my quilt *Kama* (see page 41). The usual way to finish an embroidered quilt is to tie it; see the instructions on page 37.

Techniques

Jaisalmer is where I caught the crazy patchwork bug. Just look at these colourful, richly-embellished crazy patchwork antique quilts, full of life. They often feature mirrors, and are worked in the colours of the desert.

CRAZY PATCHWORK

The use of crazy patchwork characterises many Indian wall-hangings and other pieces. The elaborate embroidery, beading and mirror-work so characteristic of needlework in the north of India is often worked on a foundation of pieced fabrics – and that patchwork is often crazy patchwork. My own work reflects this: as often as not my pieces begin with crazy patchwork, with the embellishment and the embroidered motifs coming later.

I see crazy patchwork as a basic technique, and an essential one. You can do the piecing by traditional methods or using freezer paper; I'll explain both, then you can decide which you'd rather use. One great benefit of the freezer paper method is that it makes more economical use of your fabric; you use only what's necessary for the precise shapes and their seam allowances. Whether you're working with or without freezer paper, choose a loosely-woven, lightweight foundation fabric that allows the needle to pass through easily.

Cut your foundation fabric at least 2.5-3cm (1in) larger than the intended finished size of the piece; you'll find that, just as when you're working quilting with batting/wadding, the fabric tends to 'shrink' – in this case the shrinkage is caused by close stitching. Once the block is finished and embellished, you can then trim it and cut it square and to size.

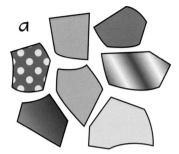

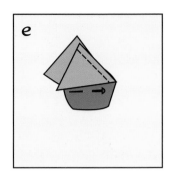

Traditional crazy patchwork

This method is worked without using freezer paper.

1 Cut fabric shapes at random (since you don't need to follow any grain lines, all kinds of scraps can be used). Vary the shapes and sizes of your patches (**a**), and cut straight lines as well as curves. Allow at least 1cm (³⁄₈in) around each edge for turnings.

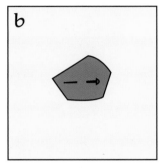

2 Choose a fabric shape with four or five sides to be your centre piece (**b**); pick a patch in a dark colour preferably, as this will draw the eye to the centre of the design and will be a good basis for later embroidery. Pin it to the centre of the foundation fabric, then take your next shape and lay it against a side of the centre piece, right sides of the fabrics together. Sew a 1cm (³⁄₈in) seam along the edge of the shape by hand or machine (**c**), turn it over to the right side, and finger-press or iron it (**d**).

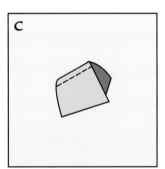

3 Take a third shape and, working clockwise, lay it against the next side of the centre piece, right sides together (**e**). Stitch the seam as before, turn over to the right side and iron or finger press (**f**). (It's important that shapes extend beyond the previous piece.) Carry on until the centre piece is surrounded (**g**). Press, and then continue working round in circuits as before until your foundation fabric is covered with shapes (**h**).

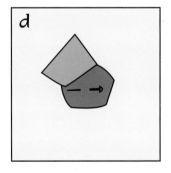

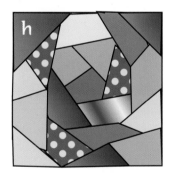

4 If you come up against an 'impossible' corner (**i**), appliqué a piece over it to rectify it (**j**). Long lines (**k**) can be shortened with curves in this same way (**l**). An awkward V-shape (**m**) can be filled with a fan-shaped patch (**n**).

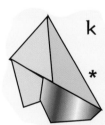

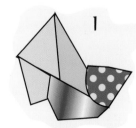

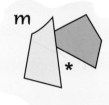

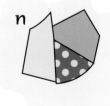

Crazy patchwork with freezer paper

An alternative way of attaching patches uses my easy freezer paper method.

1 Begin with a piece of freezer paper about 30cm (12in) square, and on the paper side, draw a range of patches in various sizes and shapes. Start with a shape with four or five sides at the centre (**a**), and work clockwise round this centre piece adding other shapes (**b**). If you prefer, you can begin drawing the paper shapes from one corner, as you can see on the diagram for the heart scatter cushion on page 95.

2 When you're happy with the shapes you've drawn onto the freezer paper, number them (**c**). Mark an asterisk (*) on the second and subsequent shapes to indicate where you want the seamlines; mark all the outside edges of the shapes with three bars (III), as shown in **d**.

3 Cut the freezer paper up into its individual numbered shapes (**e**). Iron the numbered paper shapes **on the right sides** of your selected pieces of fabric (**f**); the shiny side of the freezer paper will stick to the fabric. Cut out the fabric pieces, allowing a 2.5cm (1in) seam allowance on all sides marked III and a 1cm (⅜in) seam allowance on all the other sides (**g**).

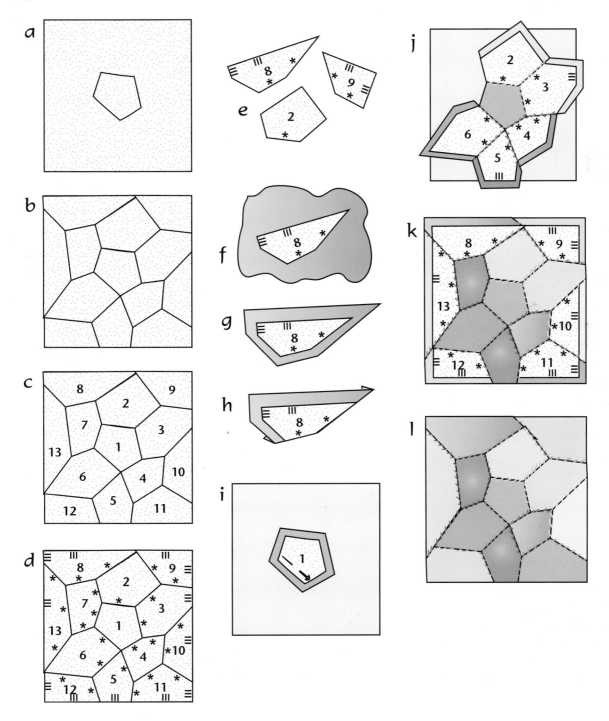

4 Turn under the edges on the seamlines marked * and press the turnings in position (**h**). Remember, an asterisk on the template always indicates that you have to fold the fabric under, and shows where this edge of the fabric patch extends over the next patch.

5 Pin piece number 1 in position on the foundation fabric (**i**). With the right sides of the patches facing up, add all the other pieces in sequence by pushing them under the other patches, then appliquéing or slipstitching (**j**). Continue adding patches in circuits, slipstitching the turned edges, until all the patches are in place (**k**). Remove the final pieces of freezer paper; you now have a square of crazy patchwork, with an overlap over your foundation square formed by the seam allowances (**l**).

TIP: If you prefer, you can stitch some of the patches in position using the 'flip and sew' method (see page 20), but this won't work if the patch has two or more sides which need to be stitched.

6 Press the finished square before you work any embroidery or embellishment.

EMBROIDERY STITCHES

Like most needleworkers I have my favourite threads and stitches, and I use these again and again. At exhibitions and workshops people tell me that they can recognise that something is my work, but as I never repeat designs, it must be something else that identifies my work. I think it must be the colours of the fabrics I use, and perhaps these favourite stitches and threads, together with the beading I love, which make my work readily recognisable. After all, if you love something and are at ease with it, you should stick with it – repeat it as often as you want, and for as long as you continue to enjoy it!

My list of favourite stitches is rather long. Each stitch is of course designed for a particular purpose, but using a range of stitches ensures variety and interest for you and for the viewer. Anyway, here's my list: herringbone (and interlaced) stitches; fly stitch; blanket and close blanket (buttonhole) stitch; Cretan stitch; chain stitch and single chain stitch (lazy daisy); open

I stayed several days in the Banni area, where the Rabari live. The Rabari men are nomads: dressed in white, they move their camels around, seeking foodstuff for them. The women, in contrast, wear black dresses; this lady has opened the top of her dress to display the highly-embroidered blouse underneath. The Rabari women are considered the best embroiderers – they love personal ornamentation, especially heavy jewellery and ear and nose rings.

chain stitch; cross stitch; stem stitch; straight stitch; feather stitches; couching stitches; French knots (for filling in); running and darning stitches.

On the following pages I'll show you how to do all these stitches, many of which are then used on the projects later on in the book, but of course you can add your own favourite stitches to the project ideas too. Note that all the diagrams for the stitches are shown from the point of view of a right-hander; if you're left-handed, work the stitches in the opposite direction.

TIP: When you're embroidering on a closely-woven fabric, a sharp needle is used; on an open-weave fabric, use a blunt-tipped tapestry needle.

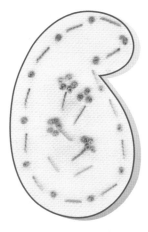
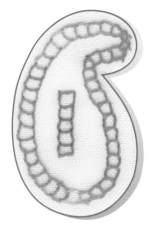
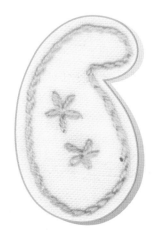

French knot

Bring the needle up at point A and wrap the thread twice round the needle (**a**). Keeping the thread taut, take the needle down at point B (**b**), as close as possible to point A but not actually into it. Hold the twists in place until the needle is completely through the fabric, to produce a small, neat knot (**c**).

Open chain stitch

Bring the needle up at point A and form a loop. Take the needle down again at B and emerge at C, bringing the needle tip over the thread (**a**). Leave the loop loose. Go down at point D, over the loop, and emerge at E for the next stitch (**b**). Anchor the end of the stitched line with two catch stitches (**c**).

Chain stitch

Bring the needle up at point A and form a loop. Go down at B (as close to A as possible, but not actually into it) and emerge at C, bringing the needle tip over the thread (**a**). Repeat this procedure to make a chain (**b**), and anchor the final loop with a catch stitch (**c**). Single chain stitches are known as 'lazy daisy', and can be built into flowers and other shapes (**d**).

a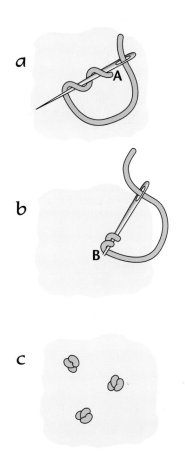

a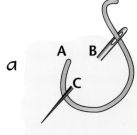

a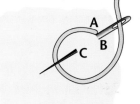

b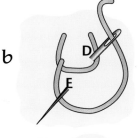

b

b

c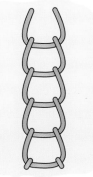

c

c

d

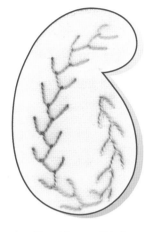
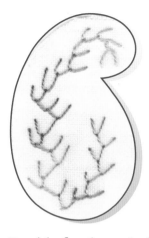

Fly stitch

Bring the needle up at point A, go down at B (level with and to the right of A), and emerge at C, bringing the needle tip over the thread (**a**). Draw the thread gently through the fabric, and take the needle down again at point D, as shown in **b**. (The position of point D depends on the length of the stitch you'd like.) When you pull the thread through, this creates a V shape caught down with a straight stitch (**c**).

Feather stitch

Bring the needle up at point A, go down at B (level with and to the left of A), and emerge at point C (**a**). Alternate the stitches back and forth on each side of the stitching line (**b**), working them downwards into a vertical column (**c**).

Double feather stitch

Work the double feather stitch in the same way as for the single feather stitch (*left*), but complete two stitches to each side of the centre line before changing the direction (**a**).

a
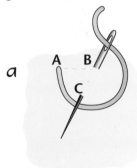

b
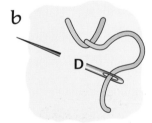

c
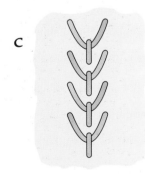

a
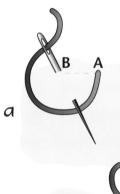

b

c
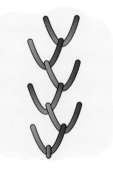

a
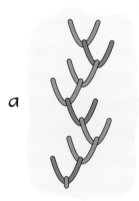

On this detail you can see both single and double feather stitches, as well as herringbone, and open chain stitch with beads.

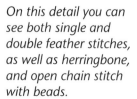

24

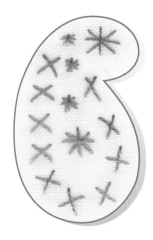
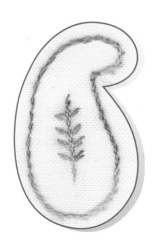

Herringbone stitch

Bring the needle up at point A, go down at B and emerge at C, making a small horizontal backstitch (**a**). Continue working in the same way, alternating stitches above and below the centre line (**b**) to create an overlapping mesh of stitches (**c**).

Cross stitch

Work cross stitches from left to right. Bring the needle up at point A, go down at B, and emerge at point C (**a**), working from lower left to upper right and making a row of evenly slanted stitches. On the return, pass each stitch from the lower right to the upper left, overlaying the first half of the stitch and forming an X (**b**).

Stem stitch

Work stem stitch along a marked line. Bring the needle up at point A (the beginning of the line) and go down at B, making a straight stitch along the stitching line; then emerge at C (the mid-point of the previous stitch) keeping the thread below the needle (**a**). Continue along the stitching line in the same way (**b**).

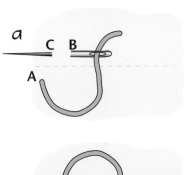
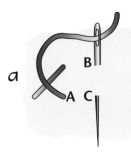
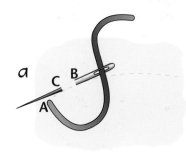

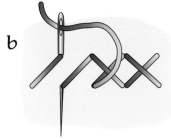

This little bird greetings card uses stem stitch in space-dyed thread to fill in a chain stitch outline.

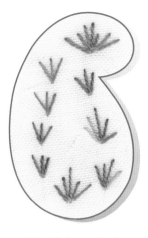 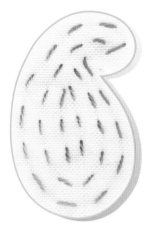 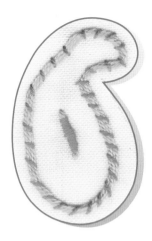

Straight stitch

Bring the needle up at point A and go down at point B (**a**), making the stitch the desired length; pull the thread through firmly so that the stitch lies flat (**b**). Straight stitches can be worked either evenly or irregularly, and can vary in length and direction.

Running stitch

Bring the needle up at point A, go down at B and emerge at point C (**a**), and continue to work the needle above and below the fabric to create a line of small, even stitches (**b**).

Couching stitch

Couching is a method used to attach a thick thread that won't go through the base fabric easily, by catching it down with small stitches in a finer thread. Work couching along a marked line; first, position the thicker thread along the line. Now, with either matching or contrasting thread, come up at A and go down at point B (**a**), wrapping a small tight stitch over the laid thread at regular intervals (**b**).

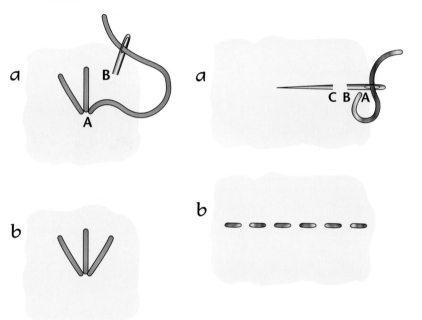

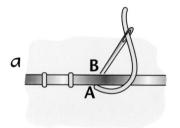

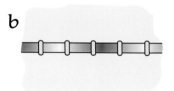

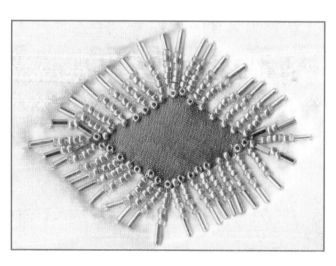

On this card design I've threaded beads onto long straight stitches to embellish a central diamond shape

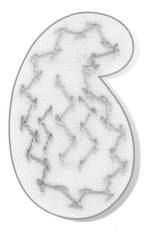

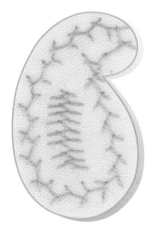

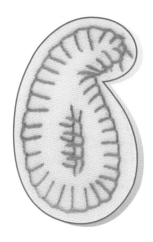

Chevron stitch

Bring the needle up at point A, go down at B and emerge at C – the centre of the stitch (**a**). Make a straight stitch the desired length to point D, insert the needle and emerge at point E (**b**). Go down at point F (the length between E and F is equal to A-B), and emerge at point G (**c**). Continue working in the same way, alternating from one side of the stitching line to the other, and keeping the stitches evenly spaced (**d**).

Cretan stitch

Bring the needle up at point A, go down at B and emerge at point C, taking a downward vertical stitch the desired length and bringing up the needle tip over the thread (**a**). Insert the needle at point D and emerge at E, taking an upward vertical stitch (**b**). Continue alternating above and below the centre line in the same way, keeping the vertical stitches evenly spaced (**c**).

Blanket stitch

Bring the needle up at point A, hold the thread down with your thumb, go down at B, and emerge at point C (**a**). Bring the needle tip over the thread and pull the stitch into place (**b**), then continue in the same way (**c**). Blanket stitches worked close together (**d**) are often known as buttonhole stitch.

a
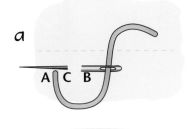

b
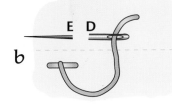

c
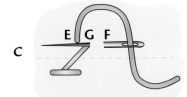

d
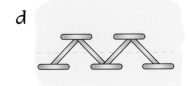

a
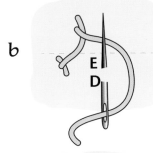

b
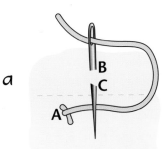

c
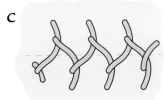

a
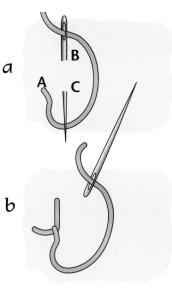

b

c
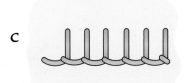

d
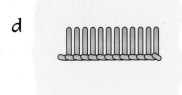

SILK RIBBON EMBROIDERY

Before I get into the techniques of ribbon embroidery, here are a few general pointers on this technique.

• I find that I use mainly 2mm, 4mm and 7mm ribbons in my work; these meet almost all the different needs, and are manageable widths.

• When using ribbons, stitch with a loose tension; this will help to create the slightly three-dimensional effect that you're looking for.

• Use a piece of ribbon 30-35cm (12-14in) long – if you use anything longer, you'll find that the ribbon wears and frays.

• A traditional knot often comes undone when you're working in rayon or silk thread, so instead use a quilter's knot with one or two twists.

• When you want to finish the stitching, use two small backstitches to secure the thread rather than tying a knot.

• Avoid the use of an embroidery hoop for bigger projects: the hoop can easily distort or crush previous ribbon stitches.

• A range of stitches from the stitch list on page 22 can be used for silk ribbon embroidery.

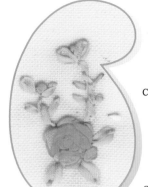

Ribbon flowers or leaves *(diagrams right)*

This is an economic way of making flowers and leaves, using half the amount of ribbon that you would need to create the same effect in lazy daisy stitch.

1 Bring the needle up through the fabric at point A. Smooth the ribbon so that it lies flat and, leaving it slack, insert the needle at point B (**a**). Pull the ribbon through until the end rolls into a point, then stop (**b**).

2 To create a flower shape, work the stitches in a circle (**c**); add French knots or beads in the centre of the flower to suggest stamens.

3 To make leaves, start by making a stem in silk thread, using stem stitch (see page 25). Then begin at the base of the stem and work ribbon stitches on alternate sides (**d**).

Spider rose
(diagrams below right)

1 Work five straight stitches in a circle to create five spokes, evenly spaced and of the same length (**a**).

2 Bring up the needle in the centre of the spokes and make a French knot (**b**).

3 Bring the needle back up to the front of the fabric, between two of the spokes and just next to the French knot. Now weave your ribbon over and under the spokes until all the spokes are covered and you've created a dense flower head (**c** and **d**). Finish off by taking the ribbon down just behind the last petal and securing it at the back of the work.

TIP: The spokes for the flower head can be made either with embroidery thread or with 4mm ribbon.

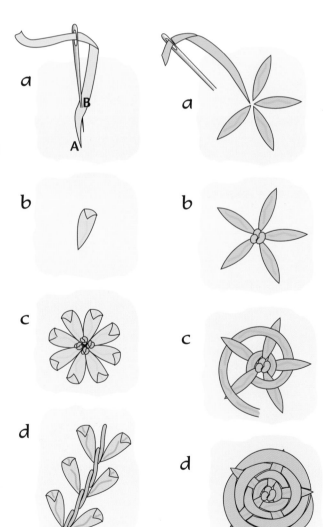

Looped flower
(diagrams below left)

1 Bring the needle up at the flower centre and smooth the ribbon so that it lies flat. Insert the needle back into the ribbon very close to the centre point (**a**). Gently pull through the loop that forms, keeping the ribbon flat; use a large needle or a cocktail stick as a 'laying tool' to keep the loop stable until it's the length you want (**b**).

2 Bring the needle up again in a new hole near the centre and repeat the process. Usually, six or seven loops make a nice flower (**c**).

3 Work French knots or add beads in the centre of the flower to create stamens (**d**).

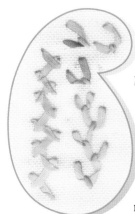

Working with other stitches
(diagrams below right)

Many other stitches (see the stitch diagrams on pages 23-27) work equally well with ribbon embroidery; herringbone stitch (**a**), feather stitch (**b**) and fly stitch (**c**) are some of the most successful.

USING MIRRORS (SHISHA)

Mirror work, or shisha (glass), gained popularity in India during the 17th century. This kind of embellishment may well have been introduced by Shah Jehan, but equally it may have entered India through Baluchistan or spread into Rajasthan and the Deccan from Gujarat. Whatever its origins, it's now an established and important technique which adds distinctive character to garments, hangings and other embroidered work. In Gujarat it's principally the women living in Kutch and Saurashtra who use mirrors in their embroidery. Nomadic peoples, especially the Rabari who travel through Rajasthan, Gujarat and the Deccan, use mirrors extensively, and the women embroider so densely around the mirrors that nothing can be seen of the background fabric.

The mirrors themselves come in a variety of shapes and sizes, but it's the round mirrors which

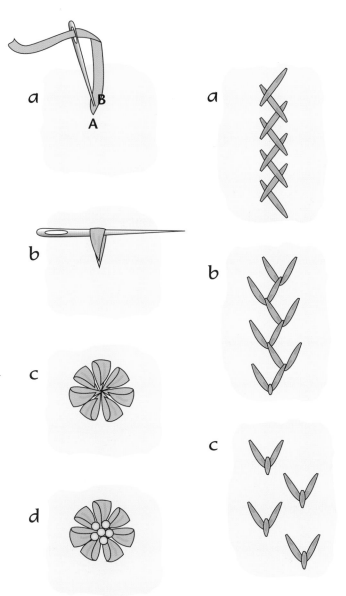

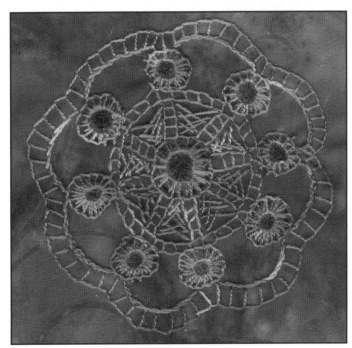

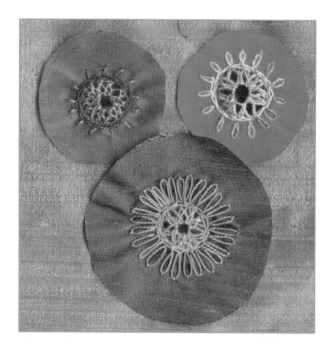

are used most commonly. The Gujarati method of affixing the mirror (*below right*) uses buttonhole stitch, while the Rajasthani method (*below centre*) uses herringbone stitch. Before the decorative embroidery is worked, whichever method is being used, the mirror is usually first held in place on the fabric with a grid of vertical and horizontal threads, worked fairly close together (see *right*).

The tension of these base stitches is critical, as they're pulled outwards to the edges of the mirror by the top stitching. If the base stitches are too loose or slack, the mirror tends to fall out; if they're too tight, it's difficult to pull the stitching out from the centre to create a satisfactory circle of stitches. A tighter tension allows more of the mirror to be shown, and the surrounding stitch becomes a fine line. A looser tension shows less of the mirror and more of its surrounding stitches.

Another method of fixing mirrors to fabric, which is becoming increasingly popular in India, uses thread-covered rings. The ring is

placed over the mirror and slipstitched into place; it's a very quick and easy method. When these rings are used, the mirror inside the frame is more noticeable, and makes a bit of a statement, whereas the stitched mirrors are somewhat more discreet.

Working the base grid *(diagrams below left)*

Work two long stitches across the mirror in one direction (**a**), then thread these with backstitches (**b** and **c**) to create a grid of stitching (**d**). This grid will hold the mirror in place while you add the decorative embroidery; it also creates a base into which you can work the top of each buttonhole or herringbone stitch.

Herringbone method *(diagrams below centre)*

Work round the mirror in herringbone stitch, working the top stitches into the grid of threads (**a**) and the bottom stitches into the fabric surround (**b**) until the edge of the mirror is completely covered (**c**).

Buttonhole stitch *(diagrams below right)*

Work round the edge of the mirror in buttonhole stitch, taking the needle into the grid of threads and taking a small stitch into the fabric each time (**a**). Continue in the same way (**b**), with the bottom of the stitches creating a line round the edge of the mirror until it's completely covered (**c**).

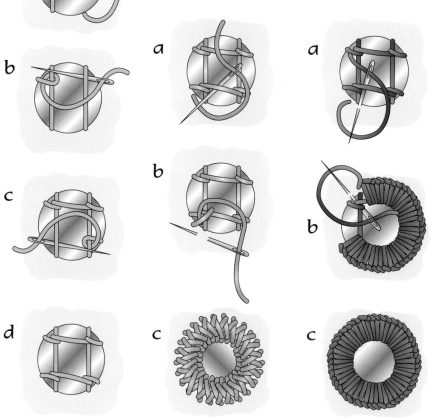

a

b

c

d

BEADWORK

Beads come in all shapes and sizes (see page 16), and they can be used to enhance and embellish Indian-style embroidery in many different ways. Beads can be stitched to the fabric individually, or couched in rows. A few tips on working with beads:

• You don't need any special equipment, although tiny seed beads and bugles require beading (or straw) needles – these are very long and fine, and can be used to couch a large number of beads at a time. In practice it's usually possible to use a fine between or appliqué needle (No 12 or 11) for all but the tiniest of beads.

• It's helpful to tip a few beads at a time into a small flat dish which has a rim; you can then pick up beads by trapping them between the point of the needle and the rim of the dish.

• If a bead gets stuck on a needle, **don't** force it over the eye – change to a smaller needle, or leave that particular bead out.

• When you're stitching on beads, use a single-strand quilting thread or a strong silk thread. Begin with a knot, and stitch back through the knot for extra security.

Couching

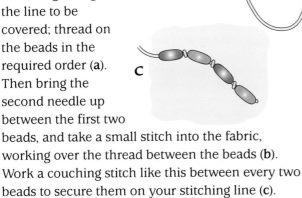

Couching is a quick way of attaching a long row of beads; you can work couching along straight or curved lines. For this technique you need to thread two needles. Secure the first length of thread at the beginning of the line to be covered; thread on the beads in the required order (**a**). Then bring the second needle up between the first two beads, and take a small stitch into the fabric, working over the thread between the beads (**b**). Work a couching stitch like this between every two beads to secure them on your stitching line (**c**).

Single beads

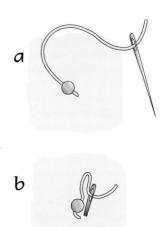

This method works for both round and bugle beads. To attach an individual bead, bring the thread up to the right side of the fabric and pick up a bead. Let the bead drop down to the end of the thread (**a**) and sew back through the fabric at the end of the bead (**b**).

Beads with embroidery

Seed beads are very good for adding texture to an otherwise flat embroidery technique. When you get to the part of the stitch where you want to use a bead, pick up a single bead on the needle (**a**) and then complete that individual stitch (**b**). Try adding a single bead onto some of the strokes of feather stitch (**c**), double feather stitch (**d**) or fly stitch (**e**).

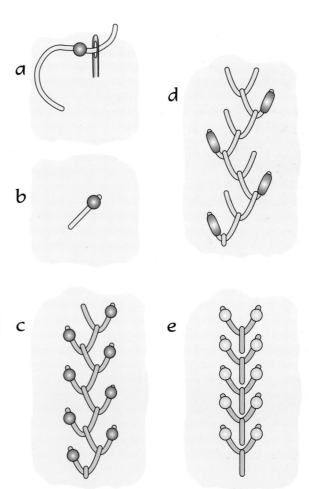

Sequins

Sequins can be attached to your fabric by securing them with a small bead.
Bring the thread up through the fabric and thread on the first sequin, followed by a small bead (**a**). Take the needle back through the hole in the sequin (**b**) and pull through; the bead holds the sequin in place and also hides the hole (**c**).

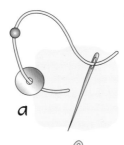

Bead picots

Little picot shapes made from beads create a pretty edging which you can use in all kinds of projects; they work well round the saddle blanket of the sumptuous standing elephant (see page 48).

Thread three beads onto your stitching thread (**a**), then work a securing stitch into the fabric that is the width of only two beads (**b**). This forces the middle bead to sit proud of the beads at the side to create a little picot shape (**c**).

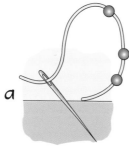

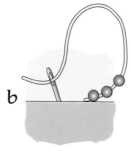

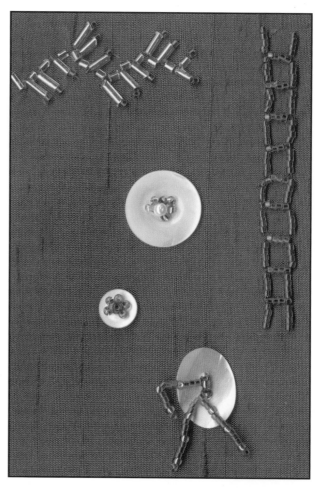

In these examples, you can see some of the many ways in which you can 'embroider' with beads, threading them onto your stitching thread before you take the different parts of each stitch.

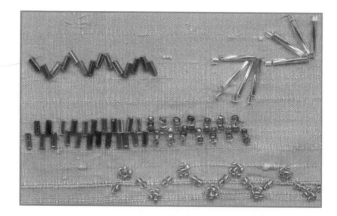

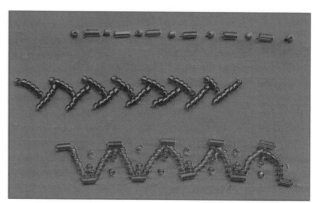

TASSELS

Tassels are versatile and useful: they can add that extra little something to your embroidery, and bring a touch of 'oomph' to your work! Well-placed tassels can bring that touch of luxury that we like to see in our homes. In some instances (for instance the kilims found in India), tassels are more than just embellishments and are an essential part of the work. The small tassels added to the edges of Qashqai kilims are to bring luck; the three special tassels hanging from a salt bag (which is quite a common item in India) are to protect its valuable contents.

These days a very wide range of tassels is available in shops, but sometimes it's not possible to get hold of exactly the size or colour, or the type of thread, that you want. The answer then is to make your own – and simple tassels are easy to make. Embroidery thread, crochet cotton and tapestry or crewel wools are all suitable for tassels; the thread you use will depend on the effect you're looking for.

These examples show just how varied tassels can be in colour, size and texture; you can decorate the head of the tassel with beads or embroidery, or make the tassel entirely out of strands threaded with beads.

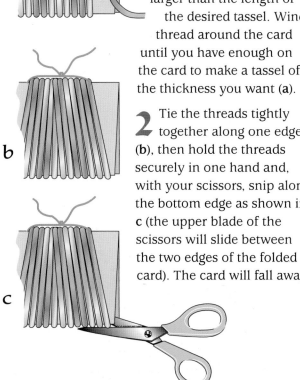

Making a simple tassel

1 Fold a piece of flexible but firm card in half, and cut it to a depth slightly larger than the length of the desired tassel. Wind thread around the card until you have enough on the card to make a tassel of the thickness you want (**a**).

2 Tie the threads tightly together along one edge (**b**), then hold the threads securely in one hand and, with your scissors, snip along the bottom edge as shown in **c** (the upper blade of the scissors will slide between the two edges of the folded card). The card will fall away.

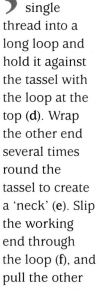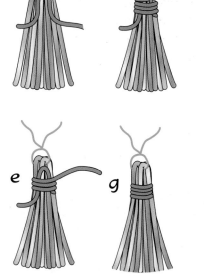

3 Fold a single thread into a long loop and hold it against the tassel with the loop at the top (**d**). Wrap the other end several times round the tassel to create a 'neck' (**e**). Slip the working end through the loop (**f**), and pull the other end to take the loop under the neck; snip the thread ends and trim the tassel neatly (**g**).

Making a ring tassel (below)

1 Work buttonhole stitch closely around a plastic or metal curtain ring (**a**). (The size of ring depends on the finished size of tassel required).

2 Cut a bunch of threads, feed them through the ring and tie them tightly together (**b**). Make a twisted cord or finger chain if you want to hang the tassel.

3 Work a row of buttonhole stitch into the head band (**c**). Carry on working round and round the head with buttonhole stitch, working into the row below each time, but **not** through the tassel head, until you reach the top (**d**).

4 Run a thread through the top row of loops, pull tightly, and secure with two or three small stitches; trim the tassel to the required length (**e**).

TIP: If you push a little padding – cotton wool or wadding – into the centre of the head, it helps to create a good, rounded shape.

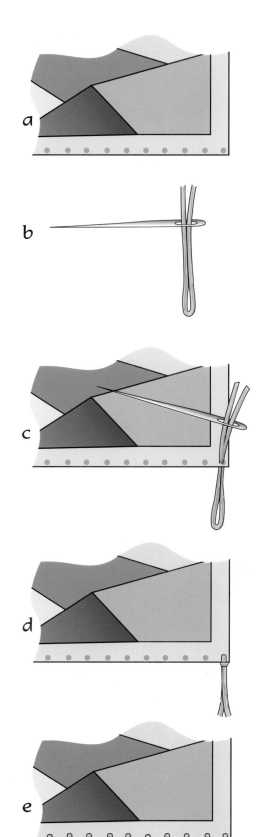

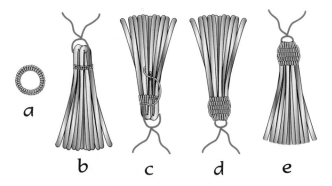

FRINGES

Fringes, like tassels, can be made rather than bought; you can create them in various ways using cotton, silk or wool, and perhaps beads, to suit your embroidery. Your final edge of loose threads can be almost any length, but it should be in balance with the depth of the knotted area of the fringe. When you're choosing a yarn and deciding on the number of threads to use, remember that the number of threads is doubled when the yarn is taken through the fabric to make a loop.

Making a simple fringe

1 Mark out the spacing of the fringe along the fabric edge of your project (**a**).

2 Cut lengths of thread twice the finished length of the fringe plus about 5cm (2in). Fold the strands for the first loop in half and thread all the

ends through a large needle (**b**). Take the needle through the fabric from the wrong side (**c**), then thread the needle through the loop and pull the knot tight (**d**).

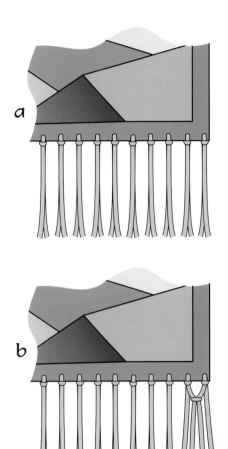
a

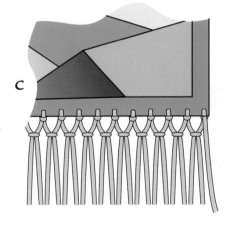
b

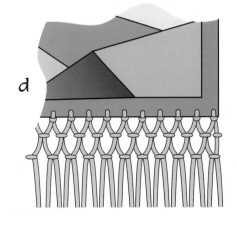
c

d

Some of the many different types of fringe that you can create to add that finishing touch to your work.

3 Repeat the process for all the other loops, to create an even fringe (**e**).

TIP: If the fabric is quite loosely woven, you can use a fine crochet hook instead of a needle for creating the fringe.

Making a knotted fringe

Remember that if you're going to knot your fringe, you'll need to make the original threads much longer; it's surprising how much thread length the knots use up.

1 Start by making a simple fringe as shown above (**a**). Divide the first and second bunches of threads into equal parts.

2 Knot the right-hand group of the first bunch with the left-hand group of the second (**b**). Repeat all the way along the work (**c**).

3 Make a knot in the loose strands (half bunches) at each end of the fringe, making sure the two knots line up with each other and with the other knots. You can work as many rows of knots as you like (**d**).

TRANSFERRING DESIGNS TO FABRIC

There are, of course, many different ways of transferring your design to your fabric; I'll explain a couple of the ones I find most useful in my work.

Using dressmaker's carbon paper

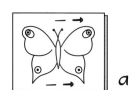

a

You need a tracing or a photocopy of your chosen design, a pencil, and special dressmaker's carbon paper. This comes in a range of colours and can be bought from most haberdasheries; you may well find that your favourite quilting supplies shop stocks it. If you're working on a light-coloured fabric, use a dark carbon paper (for instance, blue or red on cream or yellow fabric), but on a dark fabric, use a light colour of carbon paper so that it shows up (for instance, white or yellow paper on purple or jade green fabric).

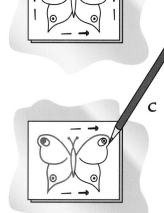

b

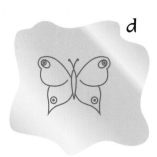

c

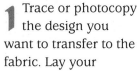

d

1 Trace or photocopy the design you want to transfer to the fabric. Lay your chosen sheet of carbon paper carbon side down, and lay the tracing or photocopy on the top, then pin the two together (**a**) to prevent 'creep' – you don't want the drawing moving while you're in the middle of transferring it.

2 Place the drawing and attached carbon paper in position on your fabric; again, you might want to put in a couple of pins to prevent movement (**b**). With a sharp, hard pencil, trace over all the lines of the design (**c**). Remove the papers, and the design will be on the fabric (**d**), ready for you to begin work.

Transferring photographs to fabric

Sometimes it's a wonderful touch to add a photograph or similar image to your quilt or wall-hanging – perhaps to feature a portrait of a friend or relative, or to show a landscape. It's now relatively easy to do this without destroying the original photograph or image. There are various specialised transfer papers which can be used in inkjet or laser printers to print out computer images, but if you don't have a computer, you can use the method below. You do need access to a colour photocopier (this method doesn't work with black and white copies or computer printouts), and you need special photo transfer paper. You also need an iron, and the fabric on which you want to reproduce the image.

Some pointers on this method, before we begin:

• Most high streets now have a print-shop which offers colour photocopying; if you don't know of one, look in your local Yellow Pages. Colour photocopies are now relatively cheap.

• The special photo transfer paper I use is American in origin; the one I've found works best is distributed by Ami Simms. Quite a few quilt shops sell the paper, so it's worth looking around.

• At first sight the sheets of transfer paper look as though they are A4 size, but in fact their measurements are slightly different, so just be aware of this discrepancy when you're using them. (A4 is 29.7 x 21cm (11⅝ x 8¼in); the transfer paper I use is 28 x 21.5cm (11 x 8½in)).

• Choose the fabric for the image carefully. The one that works best is smooth, white, closely-woven,100% cotton fabric, unwashed.

• Prepare the fabric carefully: iron it to remove moisture and creases, and remove any stray threads, lint or fibre in the area that will be receiving the image. Any blemish at this stage will appear on the finished design and will spoil the effect you want to create.

• Set your iron to the cotton setting when you're using the transfer paper, but don't use steam.

• Move the iron periodically while you're transferring the design, but lift it up and reposition it; don't slide it, as this might move the transfer paper and blur the image.

• When you're peeling the paper away from the transferred image, **don't** pull diagonally from one corner to another: pulling on the bias may distort the image.

• You can work with a single photograph, or you can build up a montage of photos on the transfer paper. If you're working with two or more individual photographs, it's wise to transfer them to the fabric one at a time.

1 Using the colour photocopier, copy the original photograph onto the transfer paper (**a**).

2 Allow at least 2.5cm (1in) of fabric all round the image – eg, for a photograph 8 x 10cm (3 x 4in), your fabric should be at least 13 x 15cm (4 x 5in). Lay the fabric right side up on the ironing board; place the transfer paper, face down, on the fabric, lining up any straight sides with the weave of the cloth (**b**).

3 Place the hot iron on the back of the transfer paper (**c**), and bear down on it as firmly as possible for 30 seconds. The harder you press, the better the resulting image.

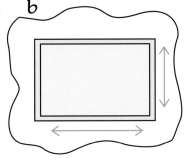

4 Remove the iron and wait 5-7 seconds to allow the paper to cool slightly and the image to bond to the fabric. Then peel off the paper, peeling from one side to the other, to reveal the image on the fabric (**d**). If the paper won't come off easily, repeat the process; the paper should come off almost clean.

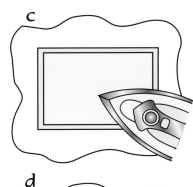

TYING

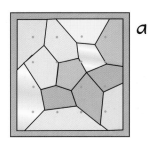

I mentioned earlier in the book that the usual way to finish an embroidered quilt is to tie it. I'm going to show you an easy way to tie quilts; this method was first demonstrated to me by Pauline Adams (who, I believe, developed it) when we were working on 'Quilts for Poland' at Hatfield House some years ago. You can work the knots on the front or the back of the work, depending on whether you want the ends of the knotted tufts to become part of the decorative front surface or prefer to have them on the reverse.

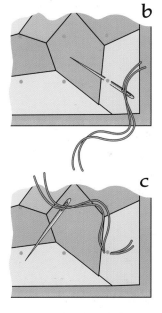

1 Mark the points for tying at about 10cm (4in) intervals (**a**). Use doubled crochet cotton or cotton knitting yarn, and a sharp, large-eyed needle. Take a stitch through all three layers (**b**), then pull the yarn up until a tail of only 5cm (2in) or so is left (**c**).

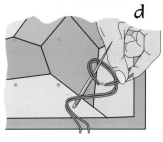

2 Loop the yarn and needle right round the back of the tail, passing the needle under and up through the front of this loop (**d**), while grabbing hold of the tail with the left hand. Pull with both hands and the knot tightens.

3 Trim the ends to leave a neat knot on the surface of the work (**e**).

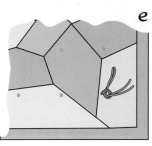

TIP: I find this method better than using reef knots; a reef knot needs a lot of 'tail' to tie it, and as a result is rather wasteful of yarn.

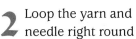

Planning and designing

Cobblers' wives showing their ari embroidery

It may seem a little cheeky for me to offer you advice on planning and designing quilts or embroidery projects, as your work will obviously be the product of your own thoughts and imagination. And yet many of us find it difficult to get started with the design process, so perhaps a few tips won't be out of place.

Thinking about what to make

You may already know what you want to make – for instance a bed quilt, a miniature, a wall-hanging, or perhaps a stuffed toy – and maybe you have some idea of the size of the finished article. For example, a small bird or cat in crazy patchwork may be only a few inches across, so the pieces of fabric you'll be working with will be correspondingly small. This size in turn influences your choice of fabrics and colours, and even the stitches you use. A large bed quilt, on the other hand, demands a different approach: the fabrics and colours must suit the style and furnishings of

the rest of the bedroom, and the precise size of the quilt will reflect the size of the bed. If the quilt is for exhibition only, your choice of design, materials and colours is likely to be quite different; you're out then to make an impression, and to display your imagination, skills and creativity.

What next?

So, having decided what you want to make, your next move is probably to think in terms of overall design and pattern. You may decide to follow a traditional path, perhaps basing your work on hexagons, or log cabin blocks, or Baltimore designs. If so, you'll find plenty of inspirational examples on show in museums and at exhibitions, and also in books; all of these will help you to envisage the finished work. Maybe by the time you reach this stage you'll also have made a decision about the techniques you'd like to use – patchwork, appliqué, trapunto, Bargello and so on. Whatever the exact order and process of your thinking, you're bound to have at the back of your mind possible fabrics and colours, and gradually a complete picture of the finished work will begin to form in your imagination.

At this stage you may decide to put your design down on paper, either working with a scale drawing or maybe just a sketch showing shapes and patterns. A drawing gives you the chance to try out the effect of colours and fabrics; if you make a few photocopies, you can try colouring the drawing in different ways, or pinning little scraps of fabric to the drawings to experiment with different colour-schemes. This process can also help to clarify what stitches, threads and so on you want to use. Drawing out a design doesn't commit you to following the drawing in every detail, of course, but it does help you to estimate what you need to make the quilt (or hanging or whatever), and to see whether you perhaps need to master any new needlework skills. Once you've done all these things, you're ready to begin your work.

Creativity, inspiration and design

Many of us (especially early on in our needlework careers) prefer to follow established paths and use familiar designs. Even with these, though, we can display some imagination in our choice of colours, shapes and fabrics. You only have to look at several Baltimore designs to see how they differ in detail while still remaining true to the essence of the Baltimore tradition. Eventually, however, our own creativity will out. Not all that many of us are genuinely original, and for most of us 'creativity' means falling in love with a particular pattern or design source, and then translating it into a work of patchwork or quilting with our own personality stamped on it.

Where you seek your inspiration will reflect your personal interests, reading, travels or chance encounters. Early on, many of my ideas came from studying and then 'personalising' the work of leading quilters, but then I began to look at buildings for inspiration, and to wander around museums looking for ideas. My hanging *Shabash*

My quilt Dhurri

was developed from the star motifs seen in the quietness of mosques and temples in Agra and Rajasthan, and *Kama* (page 41) was inspired by designs at the tomb of Mumtaz in the Taj Mahal.

Oriental carpets are a fruitful source of ideas, and were the inspiration for my *Dhurri* (above). I've always found, too, that a stroll through the galleries of the Victoria and Albert Museum in London inspires a few thoughts, as do visits to specific exhibitions – for example, the display of icons at the Royal Academy a few years ago. There can't be many museums and galleries that fail to spark an idea or two.

Focus on India

More recently, much of my work has had its roots in India, as the work in this book shows. My many visits, mainly to northern and western India, have provided me with a wealth of ideas not only as the basis of designs, but also about the use of colour, choice of fabrics and the whole field of embellishment. The extraordinary range of colours that I see in saris and other garments – some vivid, others subdued – has inevitably made me experiment more with colour in my own work, while the intricate embroidery on jackets, headwear, wall coverings and hangings has

My quilt Shabash

inspired me to incorporate its design and stitches in my own pieces. Mughal and Hindu architecture engenders ideas, too. Many of my flowers and leaf designs, particularly some I've used on borders, are based on the pietre dure designs of the great mosques; similarly, my use of beads and mirrors was inspired by the dress and hangings I saw in Gujarat and Rajasthan.

But don't think that inspiration comes only from recognised works of art. Some of the most eye-catching designs I've seen in India were on the great cloths draped over elephants, on earrings made for camels, and on boxes and cupboards in village houses. I suppose it's the unusual and the unexpected that so often give us ideas.
Many of the hangings in India are essentially crazy patchwork pieces richly embellished with mirrors, beads, even semi-precious stones, and elaborate embroidery. It's this approach which now underpins much of my work – it gives me so much scope for colour, variety of shapes, contrasts of fabrics and ornamentation that it never becomes dull. Of course elaborate patchwork, even crazy patchwork, isn't unique to India: there's a long tradition of crazy patchwork in Britain, often the product of necessity as few materials were available in poorer homes. But it's in India and other warm climates that we see it at its most extravagant.

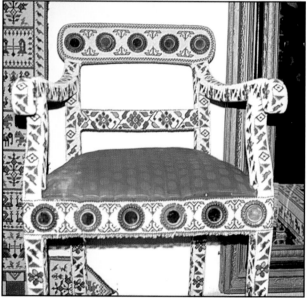

TOP: *Antique items from Gujarat; note the mirrors*
BELOW: *Chair upholstered in beads in Saurushtra*

Planning and design

We've looked at concepts and overall designs, and thought about how the world around us can give us ideas for our own work. In the case of traditional designs there are plenty of examples and patterns which we can use as the starting point for quilts and hangings, and there is also a

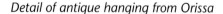

Detail of antique hanging from Orissa

wide range of stitches which most of us are familiar with, and which can be incorporated into our own projects. But as you become more adventurous, and begin to create your own designs, it's good to think about how you can record your ideas and plan the choice of colours, fabrics and, perhaps, embellishment.

In the case of a relatively straightforward crazy patchwork wall-hanging, for instance, you might have a very good idea in your mind of how it will look. Once you begin to think of colours, though, and how they harmonise, you may want to turn to pencil and paper. It's useful to sketch the design, perhaps starting with a centre-piece shape and then adding crazy shapes, moving outward from the centre, until the whole pattern or design is complete. You can then colour the various shapes, with pencils or crayons, until you feel that the design is finished.

If you've done it accurately enough you can use this drawing as a template. If not, draw the design up neatly at full size and transfer this onto your foundation fabric; you can then cut the drawing into individual pieces. These will give you the precise templates for cutting out the crazy shapes in your selected fabrics and colours, ready for appliquéing onto the foundation material. Time spent on producing a clear, accurate drawing, preferably full-size, is always time well spent; it'll save a lot of heartache later on. (You can, of course, make scale drawings if you find it easier to draw in miniature, or if your design is particularly large, but you'll have to enlarge the drawing to full size eventually to get your templates.)

Don't be afraid to alter colours, or even parts of the design, once you begin to make your quilt or hanging. The patterns are guides, not straitjackets, and what looked good on paper may not be quite so appealing when it's actually in front of you. But even if you make changes, you'll still have the pattern as a guide, and if you follow it you won't go far wrong.

An example

I gave the name of the Hindu god of love to my appliquéd quilt *Kama* (*above*), which was inspired by a motif on the cenotaph under the central cupola of the Taj Mahal (see the photograph *right*). The Taj Mahal was built by Emperor Shah Jehan as a symbol of his undying love for his wife, Mumtaz; the shimmering white marble is inlaid with with a variety of semi-precious stones – jade, onyx, cornelian and turquoise. I chose the fabrics very carefully to match the subtle shades of the original; the entire piece was worked in hand appliqué, and hand quilted.

Because the design was complex, and made up of many different elements in an elaborate arrangement, it was vital for me to create accurate full-size drawings. These drawings in turn enabled

me to cut very accurate templates – essential if the various pieces were to fit together as I did the appliqué. For this project I also felt that it was important to work some trial pieces; you can see some *below right*. I

thought that the colours on these pieces were slightly too dark, so I changed to lighter ones and a slightly different green for the final version.

Indian Bird Rope

Bird ropes are traditional in India, and are found all over the country. It's believed that hanging one in your home will bring good fortune. The designs range from the primitive to the elaborate, and can include as many as ten birds on a single rope. The birds are fun to make, and because they're small, they don't take much time – and, of course, you can make as many or as few as you want! Using three shapes to make the birds' bodies produces a crazy patchwork effect, even though in fact the shapes are far from random. You can make the birds in colours to match your decor, or as a contrast, but whatever shades you choose, these cheerful bird ropes will brighten up any room.

FOR ONE BIRD YOU WILL NEED:

✳ two pieces of foundation fabric, each at least 20 x 15cm (8 x 6in)

✳ a selection of fabrics for the 'crazy' patches (on the drawing I've suggested using three different fabrics)

✳ a small piece of soft leather or felt for the wings and beak

✳ two small black beads for the eyes

✳ a few embroidery threads and beads for embellishment

✳ co-ordinating thread for sewing

✳ thick thread for the 'rope' (I used coton perlé No 5)

✳ scissors

* a few larger beads, bells, etc for decorating the hanging rope
* cardboard for the templates, and a craft knife or scissors for cutting the card
* a large bodkin or trapunto needle
* coloured marker pen

I find it useful to make templates for the three patchwork fabrics, marked C, D and E on the pattern. Where the outer edges of the bird are marked III, I allow 1cm (½in) overlap of material on all the marked edges. An asterisk (*) on a template indicates where you have to fold the edge of the fabric to the wrong side, and where the edge of one fabric patch overlaps another.

STEP BY STEP

1 Trace or photocopy shapes **A, B, C, D, E** and **F** on page 89 and stick them onto card; cut them out to make templates. Lay one piece of foundation fabric right side down and position the main bird template (A) on top; with a coloured marker, draw round the outline (**a**). Then turn the material right side up and use the template to draw another bird outline so that it coincides exactly with the first. (This second outline will help when you've covered one side of the fabric with your crazy patches; it will act as a guide when you're ready to line and back your bird.) Cut the shape out, adding a generous seam allowance.

2 Use templates C, D and E to cut three shapes from your fabrics (**b**), remembering to add 1-1.5 cm (⅜-½in) seam allowance around each edge.

3 Cover the foundation shape with your assortment of materials. Start by pinning on shape C, then take shape D, fold the material over where the asterisk (*) is marked, and sew this to the first patch using slipstitch or appliqué stitch (**c**). Repeat the process with the remaining patch (**d**). One side of the bird is now finished.

4 Now repeat the entire process from step 1 with the other piece of foundation fabric, working with the templates the other way round, to create the second half of the bird as a mirror image (**e**). Remember that you'll need to use templates C-E in reverse as well as the main bird shape.

5 You now have two pieces of foundation fabric with the bird shape worked in crazy patchwork on each. Embroider and embellish over the seam lines using feather stitch and fly stitch (see page 24) with beads attached at the tips of the stitches (see page 31).

6 With right sides facing, put the two sections of the bird together and sew by hand or machine all the way around the marked lines, leaving a gap for turning (**f**). Clip round all the angles – especially the ones round the tail – to make the shape easier to turn out. Once the bird shape is right side out, stuff it firmly, then use slipstitch to close the gap in the seam (**g**).

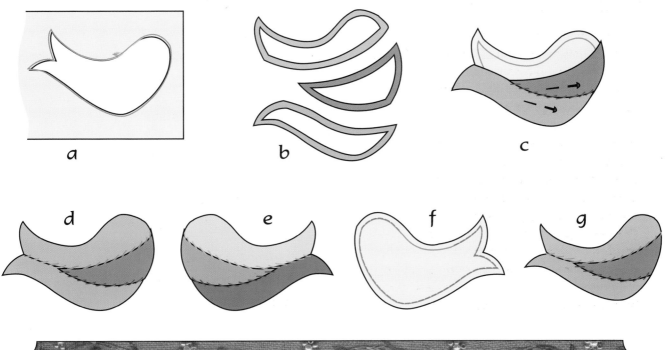

a

b

c

d

e

f

g

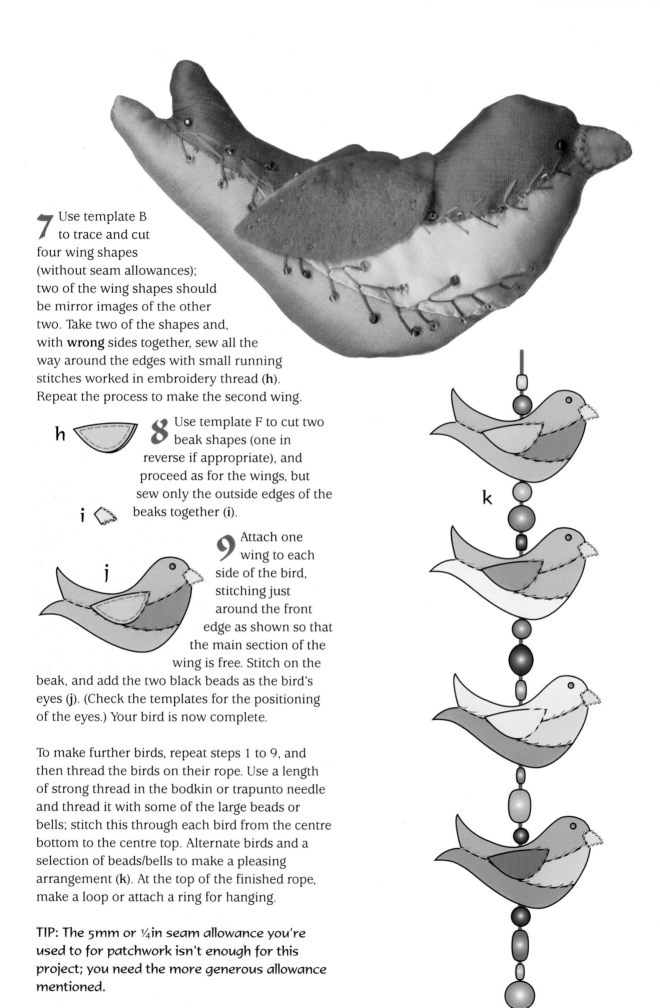

7 Use template B to trace and cut four wing shapes (without seam allowances); two of the wing shapes should be mirror images of the other two. Take two of the shapes and, with **wrong** sides together, sew all the way around the edges with small running stitches worked in embroidery thread (**h**). Repeat the process to make the second wing.

h

8 Use template F to cut two beak shapes (one in reverse if appropriate), and proceed as for the wings, but sew only the outside edges of the beaks together (**i**).

i

9 Attach one wing to each side of the bird, stitching just around the front edge as shown so that the main section of the wing is free. Stitch on the beak, and add the two black beads as the bird's eyes (**j**). (Check the templates for the positioning of the eyes.) Your bird is now complete.

j

k

To make further birds, repeat steps 1 to 9, and then thread the birds on their rope. Use a length of strong thread in the bodkin or trapunto needle and thread it with some of the large beads or bells; stitch this through each bird from the centre bottom to the centre top. Alternate birds and a selection of beads/bells to make a pleasing arrangement (**k**). At the top of the finished rope, make a loop or attach a ring for hanging.

TIP: *The 5mm or ¼in seam allowance you're used to for patchwork isn't enough for this project; you need the more generous allowance mentioned.*

Hanging Elephant

Just as you find traditional bird ropes throughout India, so you'll also find ropes of hanging elephants. The elephant ropes are often sewn by village children as they make their first attempts at creativity, and the older children decorate them beautifully from head to foot; the animals are usually made from old saris and stuffed with cut-up pieces of cotton fabric. Very often the rope has a bell attached to the bottom end – perhaps a reminder of the Hindu practice of ringing the bell over the entrance to a temple to let the deity know of the visit.

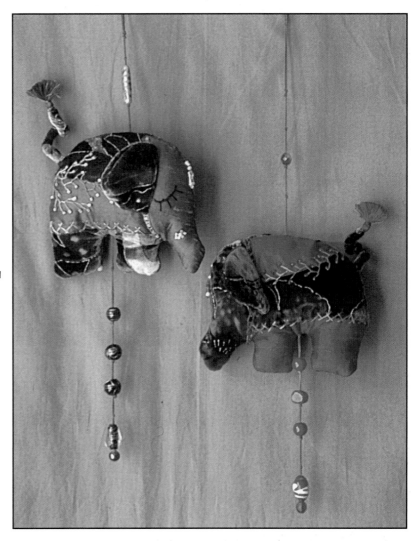

YOU WILL NEED:

✳ cardboard for creating the templates

✳ foundation fabric, at least 30 x 22cm (12 x 9in)

✳ small patches of sumptuous fabrics for the crazy patches, the ears and the tail (you can use all the off-cuts you end up with in your work-basket – just go through your odds and ends)

✳ a piece of pipe cleaner

✳ embroidery floss and other threads for embroidering/embellishing over all the seams and for stitching the eyes

✳ beads and bugle beads, mirrors and any other embellishments you fancy

✳ matching thread and needles (for beading I use No 11 or No 12 appliqué needles)

✳ paper and fabric scissors

✳ wadding for stuffing the elephant

✳ bodkin or trapunto needle

✳ coton perlé for the hanging 'string'

✳ an assortment of beads or bells for decorating the string

✳ coloured marker pen

STEP BY STEP

1 Trace or photocopy shapes **A**, **B**, **C**, **D**, **E**, **F** and **G** on page 90, then stick them onto the cardboard and cut the shapes out to create templates. Place the main elephant template over the foundation fabric and, with a coloured marker, draw round the outline (see diagram **a** on page 47). Then turn the material to the other side and, reversing the template, draw a second elephant outline that coincides exactly with the first. This outline on the back helps you when you've covered the front of the fabric with crazy patches – it gives you an accurate guide on the wrong side when you're ready to line and back your elephant. Cut out the patches, leaving a generous seam allowance all the way around (**b**).

2 Cut patches from your sumptuous fabrics, always adding 1-1.5cm (³/₈-¹/₂in) seam allowance to each edge. (The 5mm/¹/₄in seam allowance used for ordinary patchwork is not enough.)

3 Following the instructions for crazy patchwork on page 20, cover the elephant shape on the right side of the foundation fabric with an assortment of fabric patches (**c**). Start with the leg section (template C) and work through shapes D, E and F.

4 With large tacking stitches, outline the shape of the elephant on the back of the foundation fabric. Trim all overhanging fabric away, leaving only a 1cm (³/₈-¹/₂in) seam allowance all round.

5 Now embroider and embellish your elephant (**d**). You can use some of the stitches from my stitch list on page 22, or, if you prefer, just use one stitch throughout. There's no absolute rule in crazy patchwork! Embroider the eye using blanket stitch or straight stitches.

6 Follow exactly the same method, from step 1, to create a second crazy patchwork shape which is a mirror image of the first (**e**). Remember to use templates C-F in reverse as well as the main elephant shape.

7 Using template B, mark four shapes (two in reverse) and cut them out, adding seam allowances all the way around. Take one pair of ear shapes and, with right sides facing, stitch round the marked outline, leaving a gap on the straight edge for turning (**f**). Turn right side out and close the ear with small stitches; press it, and sew it to the embellished elephant (**g**), checking the position on the template. Do the same for the second ear and sew it to the other side of the elephant.

8 For the tail, use template G to cut a piece of fabric on the bias; the seam allowance is included on this template. Fold this piece lengthways, right sides together, then sew along the long side and one of the short sides to produce a narrow tube (**h**). Turn this right side out (be patient here – I often use a pencil to aid the process) and insert a pipe-cleaner (**i**). Pin the tail to one of the sides of the elephant at the point shown on the template (**j**).

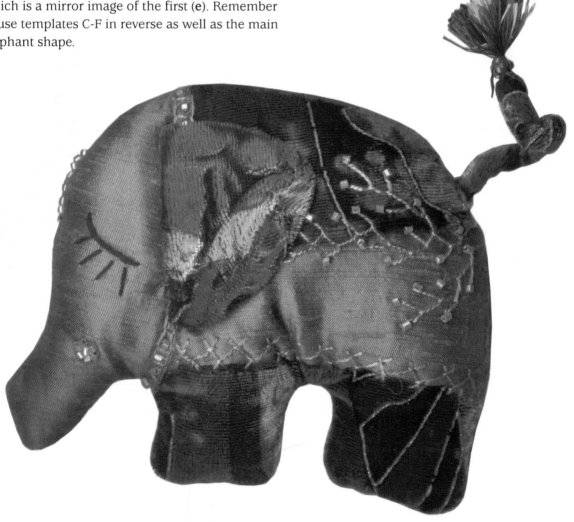

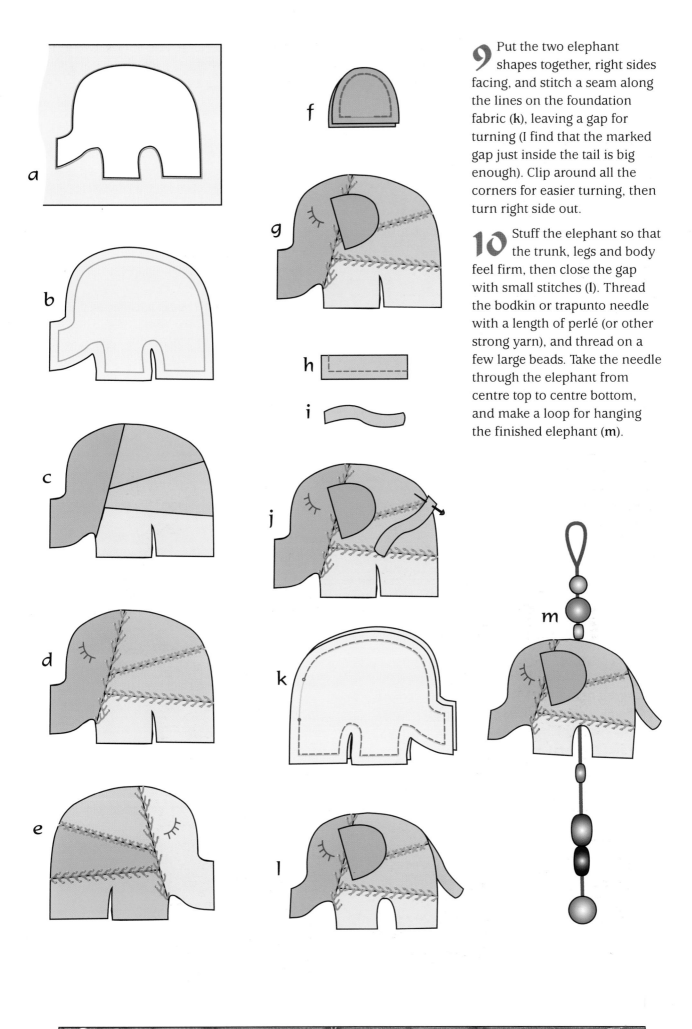

9 Put the two elephant shapes together, right sides facing, and stitch a seam along the lines on the foundation fabric (**k**), leaving a gap for turning (I find that the marked gap just inside the tail is big enough). Clip around all the corners for easier turning, then turn right side out.

10 Stuff the elephant so that the trunk, legs and body feel firm, then close the gap with small stitches (**l**). Thread the bodkin or trapunto needle with a length of perlé (or other strong yarn), and thread on a few large beads. Take the needle through the elephant from centre top to centre bottom, and make a loop for hanging the finished elephant (**m**).

Sumptuous Standing Elephant

You find elephant figures wherever you go in India; sometimes they're made of silver or papier maché, sometimes of wood, stone or marble. They're frequently adorned with beautiful coloured bindis (marks on the forehead) and always have highly-decorated saddle-blankets. My little standing elephants evolved from the hanging ones (see page 45), and I decorate each one elaborately with beaded fringes on the saddle-blanket and forehead, and a silk tassel on the tail.

Add a 1cm (⅜-½in) seam allowance around all the edges of each patch as you cut the fabric shapes out, except for the feet and trunk pads, which are cut out without seam allowances.

YOU WILL NEED:
* foundation fabric at least 50 x 22cm (20 x 9in); a fat quarter is enough for two elephants
* sumptuous fabric (velvet, brocade, silk etc) for the elephant, the gusset, the ears and the tail – roughly 35 x 40cm (14 x 16in)
* contrasting fabric for the saddle blanket, roughly 20 x15cm (8 x 6in)
* small piece of felt or thin wash-leather for the five pads
* cardboard for creating the templates
* piece of pipe cleaner for inserting into the tail
* black cotton embroidery thread for the eyes
* beads and bugle beads for the fringe and surround on the saddle blanket
* special large beads, or any other decorations you have, for the middle of the saddle blanket and for attaching to the head
* a few extra beads for attaching to the body of the elephant (optional)
* matching threads and needles (for beading I use No 11 or No 12 appliqué needles)
* paper and fabric scissors
* wadding to stuff the elephant when finished
* coloured marker pen

STEP BY STEP

1 Trace or photocopy shapes **A**, **B**, **C**, **D**, **E**, **F** and **G** on page 91, then stick them onto the cardboard and cut the shapes out to create templates. Following the instructions on page 45, mark two whole elephant shapes (template A) and one gusset shape (template B) on both sides of the foundation fabric with a coloured marker. Cut out the patches, leaving a generous seam allowance all the way around (**a**).

TIP: You need two elephant shapes on the foundation fabric and cut from the main fabric, one as a mirror image of the other, so you might find it easier to make two separate templates to remind you.

2 Use the elephant template(s) and the gusset template to cut shapes from your chosen sumptuous fabric, remembering to add the seam allowances. Lay these shapes right side up on their corresponding patches in foundation fabric, and work a line of tacking/running stitches along the lines marked on the back of the foundation patches to secure them in place (**b**).

3 Use template E to cut two patches (mirror images) from the saddle blanket fabric, adding seam allowances (**c**). Turn the seam allowances to the back round the sides and bottom edges of the shapes; lay them right side up on the elephant shapes as indicated on the template, and slipstitch them in position round the turned edges (**d**).

4 Now it's time to decorate the saddle blanket. Attach beads and bugle beads around the blanket one by one (**e**) – or, if you prefer, make picot shapes with beads (see page 32).

5 Embroider the lines of the eyes and eyelashes, using either blanket stitch or straight stitches.

6 Use template C to mark out four ear shapes, two in reverse; cut them out, adding the seam allowances. Take two mirror image shapes and, with right sides facing, sew over the marked outline, leaving a gap on the straight edge for turning (**f**). Turn right side out, and close the opening with small stitches; press, then sew the ear onto one side of the embellished elephant, checking the position on the template (**g**). Do the same for the second ear and sew it on to the other side of the elephant.

7 Follow the instructions on page

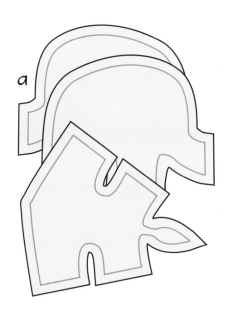

a

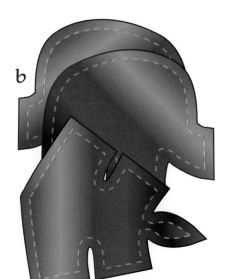

b

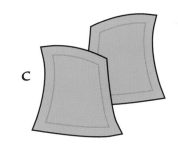

c

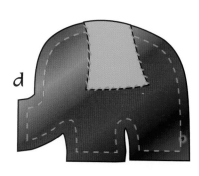

d

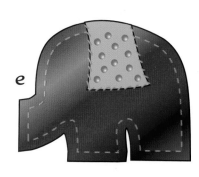

e

f

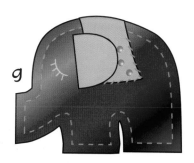

g

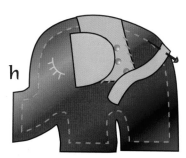

h

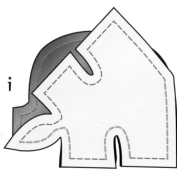

i

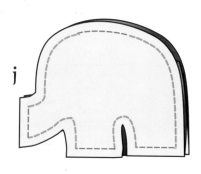

j

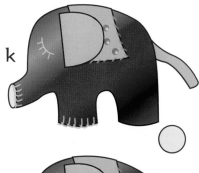

k

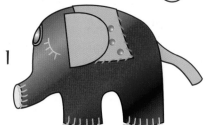

l

46 to create the tail and pin it in position (**h**).

8 With right sides together, pin and stitch the gusset piece to the sides of the elephant, leaving gaps for the feet (**i**). Now stitch the top edges of the elephant sides together, leaving a gap for the tip of the trunk and another at the top for turning (**j**).

TIP: *Make absolutely sure that the pipe cleaner inside the channel is well sewn into the seam line of the elephant, so that you can manipulate the tail into shape when the elephant is finished.*

9 Turn the elephant shape right way out through the top opening. Cut the five circles (four from template F for the foot pads, one from template G for the tip of the trunk) and sew these in position with buttonhole stitch (**k**).

10 Stuff the elephant shape so that the legs and body have a firm feel, then close the gap with small stitches. Add some beads or an Indian bindi fixed to the front of the head (**l**). As an optional extra, make a small tassel for the end of the tail; it gives the elephant a nice finishing touch.

BELOW: *Some of the lovely decorative bindis that you can buy in India.*

Embroidered Cards

Making your own greetings cards is rewarding, as well as good fun. They're a very personal way of saying thank you, or of sending good wishes or celebrating a birthday, and they aren't difficult to make; they just require a little care and patience. You can buy the card blanks themselves in many different places – from quilt shops and stationers', and at shows and exhibitions. The blanks come in a wide range of sizes, colours and textures, and have apertures of different sizes and shapes, including novelty shapes such as hearts and teddy bears; if you're a beginner, you'll find that the rectangular, circular and oval apertures are the most straightforward to work with.

Choosing the embroidery design to go on your home-made card needs a bit of care. You need to bear in mind the embroidery motif itself, the colour and texture of the background

fabric, the size of the design, the various threads you want to use, the size and colour of the card, and the size and shape of the aperture. Sometimes it's easier to pick the card blank you want to use and then choose your embroidery motif to suit it, rather than the other way around. (Mind you, if you're really adventurous you can design and make your own card from suitable fabric.)

In this section I've given you designs and instructions for five different embroidered cards, all of which are easy to stitch and assemble. The motifs are quite different, and are designed to suit cards of different shapes and sizes, but all five use exactly the same basic assembly technique. I've also included photographs of a couple of other designs that would be easy to copy, and any of the motifs that I used on Country Concerto (see pages 80 and 107-110) would work well on cards too.

The tulip design looks good in a card with a large circular aperture; the flowers and leaves are worked in bright space-dyed threads. The peacock and elephant designs fit into slightly smaller circles. I designed the bouquet motif to fit into a gold card mount with an oval aperture, and added a few beads to the design for extra sparkle. The final design is an Indian-style flower motif, which fits in a card mount with a square aperture; I've embellished this design with gold and pearl beads.

TIPS: For each design I've used a No 8 crewel embroidery needle, and small sharp scissors for trimming the fabric and wadding. I've also specified a large piece of background fabric; this is so that, if you wish, you can mount it in an embroidery frame while you're working the embroidery; it can be trimmed down to size once all the embellishment is complete. For each design you'll also need some double-sided sticky tape. The templates for all the card designs are on page 92.

YOU WILL NEED:

FOR THE TULIP DESIGN
* card blank in your chosen colour with a circular aperture 10cm (4in) in diameter
* background fabric 18cm (7in) square
* embroidery thread in two or three colours, preferably space-dyed
* piece of wadding the size of the folded card blank

FOR THE ELEPHANT DESIGN
* card blank in your chosen colour with a circular aperture 9.5cm (3½in) in diameter
* background fabric 15cm (6in) square
* grey embroidery thread for the body of the elephant
* multi-coloured threads for the saddle blanket, headpiece and toes, and for the small dots on the body
* black thread for the elephant outline and for the eye
* piece of wadding the size of the card

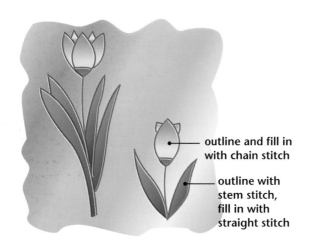

outline and fill in with chain stitch

outline with stem stitch, fill in with straight stitch

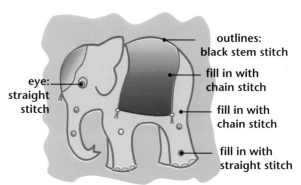

eye: straight stitch

outlines: black stem stitch

fill in with chain stitch

fill in with chain stitch

fill in with straight stitch

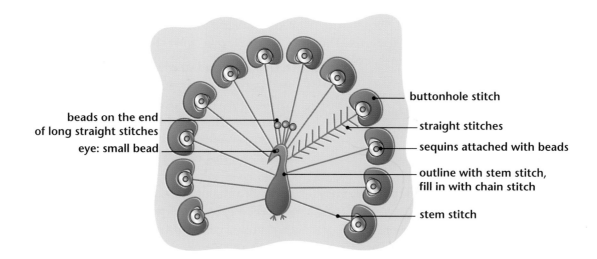

beads on the end of long straight stitches

eye: small bead

buttonhole stitch

straight stitches

sequins attached with beads

outline with stem stitch, fill in with chain stitch

stem stitch

FOR THE PEACOCK DESIGN

* card blank in your chosen colour with a circular aperture 9.5cm (3½in) in diameter
* background fabric 15cm (6in) square
* suitable peacock-coloured space-dyed thread for the body and feathers
* 12 small sequins
* 12 small beads for attaching the sequins
* 3 small beads for the plumes
* small bead for the eye (or work a French knot)
* piece of wadding the size of the card
* appliqué needle No 11 or 12

FOR THE BOUQUET DESIGN

* card blank in your chosen colour with an oval aperture 8 x 10cm (3¼ x 4in)
* fabric 10 x 14cm (4 x 5½in) for the embroidery
* variegated embroidery thread
* a few small beads
* a piece of wadding the size of the card
* appliqué needle No 11 or 12

FOR THE INDIAN FLOWER DESIGN

* card blank in your chosen colour with a 6cm (2½in) square aperture
* fabric for the embroidery 12cm (5in) square
* embroidery thread in off-white
* 9 pearls
* approximately 30 gold beads
* piece of wadding the size of the card
* appliqué needle No 11 or 12

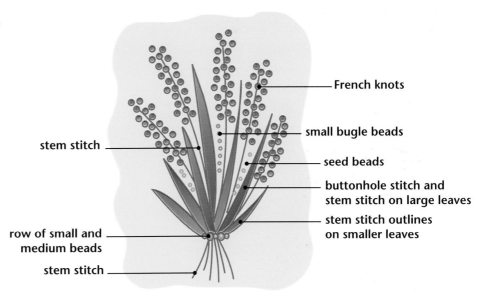

French knots

small bugle beads

seed beads

buttonhole stitch and stem stitch on large leaves

stem stitch outlines on smaller leaves

stem stitch

row of small and medium beads

stem stitch

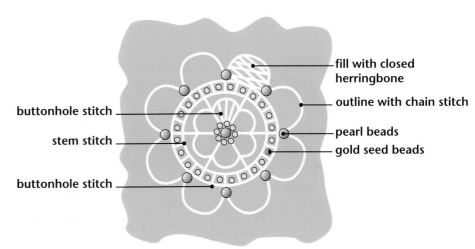

fill with closed herringbone

outline with chain stitch

buttonhole stitch

stem stitch

pearl beads

gold seed beads

buttonhole stitch

STEP BY STEP

Each card is worked and then assembled in the same way.

1 Choose the design you want to use from page 92; transfer this onto the background fabric (**a**), either by tracing or by using dressmaker's carbon paper (see page 36).

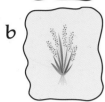

2 Following the stitching guidelines shown on the colour drawings, embroider the design (**b**) and add any embellishments. Iron the finished design very lightly on the back (this is particularly important if you used a hoop, because it might have left a mark on the fabric).

3 Unfold the card blank so that the aperture is in the centre and there's a flap on each side: lay it face down on your work surface (**c**). Cut small pieces of double-sided tape and stick them round the aperture (**d**).

4 Lay the embroidery over the aperture, **right** side down, making absolutely certain that the motif or design is in the centre (**e**). Peel the backing papers off the pieces of tape and press the embroidered fabric firmly into place, taking care to keep it centred in the aperture.

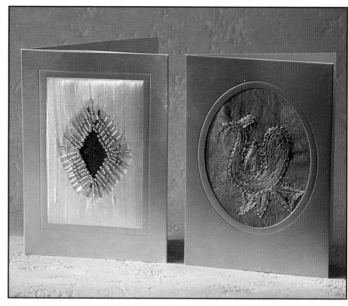

Simple geometric designs and animal and bird motifs, embroidered and embellished, also work well as cards

5 With the card still face down, fold over the left-hand flap; trim away any surplus fabric that extends beyond the flap (**f**). Unfold the flap again, then put strips of double-sided tape round all four edges of the middle (aperture) panel (**g**).

6 Lay the piece of thin wadding over the centre of the fabric, peel the backing papers off the pieces of tape, and fold the left-hand flap back over the centre panel (**h**); press it firmly in place. Your card is now finished (**i**).

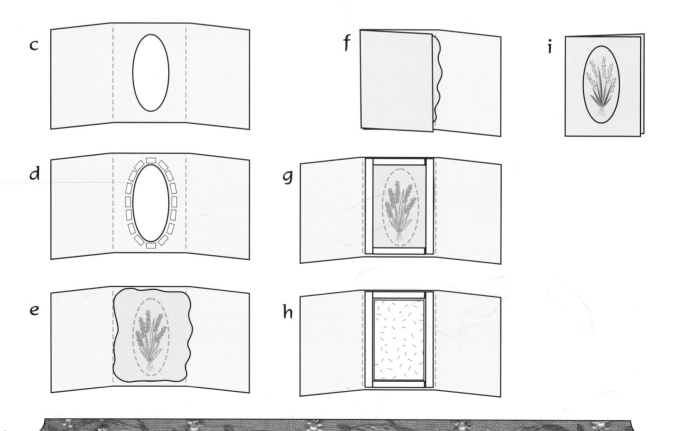

Evening Bag

Hindus revere the peacock, and peacock details adorn richly-painted archways, especially in Rajasthan, where the peacock is the emblem of the state. It's an ancient Indian belief that peacocks prophesy the coming of the monsoon; their ritual courtship takes place just before the onset of the monsoon rains. The peahen is a brown and somewhat drab creature, but the cock bears a magnificent 'train' and highly-coloured plumage.

The bag is made in three stages. The first task is to assemble and prepare the different materials (fabric, lining and wadding). The lining actually creates a border at the top of the bag, so choose a good-quality fabric that is a contrast to your main fabric; I used a lime green shot silk for the bag and a jade green silk for the lining. Next, embroider the peacock motif onto the front panel; once you've done this, you're ready for the final stage, which is to assemble and line the bag.

YOU WILL NEED:

FOR THE BAG

* fabric for the front and back, two pieces each measuring 20 x 23cm (8 x 9in)
* contrast fabric for the lining, two pieces as above
* lightweight polyester wadding, two pieces as above
* 1m (40in) strong cord or braid for the shoulder strap
* 50cm (20in) of belt backing (something like petersham would be fine), 2.5cm (1in) wide
* large popper/press stud
* thread to match the fabric

FOR THE EMBROIDERY

* skein of 12-ply space-dyed embroidery silk
* skein of Anchor lamé embroidery thread in gold (or similar)
* 39 green sequins and 39 small green beads
* 4 medium green beads for the plumes on the peacock's head
* tracing paper
* dressmaker's carbon paper
* hard, sharp pencil
* extra sequins and beads for decorating the bag top (optional)

STEP BY STEP

TO WORK THE EMBROIDERY

1 Trace or photocopy the drawing of the peacock on page 93. Lay the fabric which will form the front of the bag right side up; using dressmaker's carbon paper (see page 36), transfer the design to the fabric (**a**).

2 To embroider the peacock, outline the body in chain stitch (see page 23), using one or two strands of the 12-ply thread. Fill in the body with chain stitch (**b**).

3 With two strands of gold lamé, and working in stem stitch (see page 25), embroider all the central 'spines' of the feathers (**c**). For the main parts of the feathers themselves use straight stitches, working with one or two strands of 12-ply thread (**d**).

4 Use buttonhole or blanket stitch (see page 27) in a fan design to create the 'eyes' at the tops of the feathers; on the inside of each fan work an outline in stem stitch (**e**).

5 Add three green sequins in each of the tail's eyes, securing each sequin with a small green bead (**f**). The beak and the eye are worked in gold lamé.

6 Work a few small straight stitches underneath the body to suggest feet, and work four straight stitches at the top of the head to create plumes. Add one medium green bead to each of the plumes (**g**).

TO ASSEMBLE THE BAG

TIP: When you're making the bag, stitch all seams with the right sides of fabric together, and use a 1.5cm (½in) seam allowance unless otherwise stated.

1 Take the embroidered front piece of fabric, and the matching fabric which will form the back of the bag, and tack/baste a rectangle of wadding to the wrong side of each patch (**h**).

2 Pin these two fabric patches right sides together and stitch a seam around the sides and bottom, stitching in a curve round corners and leaving the top open (**i**). Trim away the excess seam allowance at the bottom corners (**j**).

3 Turn the bag right side out. Pin the strap at the top of the side seams, right sides facing and matching the raw edges, and tack in place (**k**).

4 Cut two 18cm (7in) long pieces of belt backing. Take the two pieces of lining fabric and lay them right sides up; position a piece of the belt backing 2cm (¾in) below the top edge of each fabric patch, making sure that it's in the middle, and stitch in place. (This helps to

a

b

c

e

d

f

stiffen the top of the bag.) Pin and stitch the two pieces of lining together, leaving the top edges open and leaving a gap in the lower edge for turning through (**l**).

5 Matching the side seams, pin and stitch the lining to the bag around the top edge of the shoulder strap (**m**).

6 Turn the lining right side out; sew up the gap, and push the lining down inside the bag. Because of the positioning of the belt backing, this will create a little border of the lining fabric at the top of the bag (**n**); if you wish, you can decorate the edge of this border with more sequins and beads. Sew the popper/press stud to the top edges to fasten the bag.

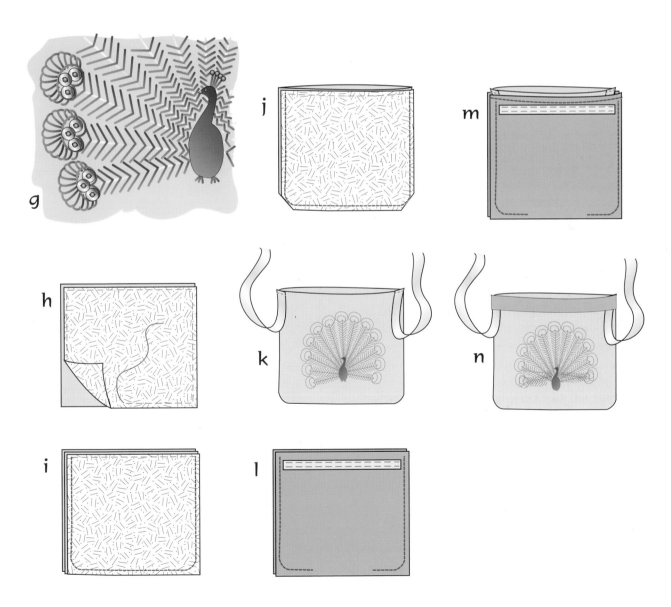

Chain Stitch Sampler

I did most of the stitching on my first version of this sampler sitting outside a hut in Gujarat, although I had to finish it once I was back home in England. I was in Gujarat for several days, and during this time I sat with the local embroiderers, studying their techniques. They gave me a piece of black cotton fabric and a handful of coloured threads which looked like our six-stranded embroidery threads; I used two strands of each colour at a time, working in chain stitch round and round the shapes I'd drawn on the background fabric. It was hot (the temperature was well over 35° centigrade), and I was flat on my bottom, on the baked mud surface in front of the hut.

YOU WILL NEED:
* cotton fabric, roughly 30cm (12in) square
* backing fabric the same size
* 10-12 different colours of stranded embroidery threads
* embroidery needle (crewel No 7 or 8 works well)
* embroidery hoop (optional)
* dressmaker's carbon paper
* hard, sharp pencil

STEP BY STEP

1 Photocopy the design for the sampler on page 94, enlarging it to the correct size. Using dressmaker's carbon paper (see page 36), transfer all the lines of the design to your fabric (a).

2 Choose one of the outside rectangles and begin your embroidery on that shape. Outline the shape with a circuit of chain stitch (b), then work a second line inside the first, and continue in the same way. Make the chain stitches the same length in each circuit, but reduce the number of stitches each time; this creates a rather pleasing mitred effect in the corner of each shape. Work the rows of chain stitch snugly up against each other; this prevents the background fabric from peeping through. When you get to the inner shape, change to a different colour and continue in the same way (c).

3 Move on to one of the neighbouring blocks and fill it in the same way but using different colours; work your way across the whole design using the same method (**d**). If you prefer, you can alter the colours more frequently within some of the blocks, using perhaps three or four different colours, as shown in the detail (*right*).

4 Once all the shapes are filled, surround the whole design with a row of chain stitch to give it a little border (**e**).

5 You can finish off the sampler by backing it with a piece of fabric the same size to create a mat or a decorative panel. If you'd like to use the design as a cushion cover, begin with a 40cm (16in) square and back it with a similar-sized piece before slipping in the cushion pad. In either case, choose a backing fabric that complements the colours of your stitchery.

TIP: **You won't need whole skeins of stranded embroidery thread to produce one sampler; I use up odds and ends.**

a

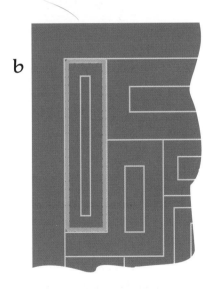

b

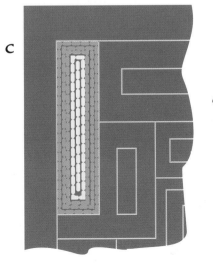

c

d

e

Scatter Cushions

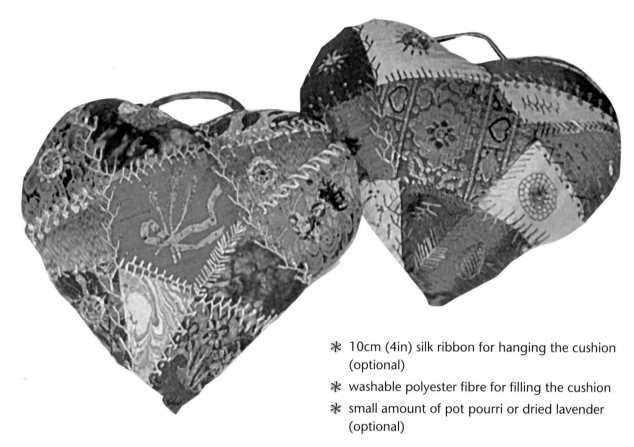

* 10cm (4in) silk ribbon for hanging the cushion (optional)
* washable polyester fibre for filling the cushion
* small amount of pot pourri or dried lavender (optional)

These romantic-looking crazy patchwork cushions are quite small, with a finished size of roughly 20cm (8in) square, so this design is a good project for trying out freezer paper crazy patchwork (see page 21) if you haven't attempted it before. You could turn the design into a scented herb cushion by adding some pot pourri or dried lavender along with the stuffing.

YOU WILL NEED:
* foundation fabric, 25cm (10in) square
* fabric for the back of the cushion, 25cm (10in) square
* selection of different fabrics for the crazy patches
* matching thread
* embroidery threads
* beads, sequins, mirrors, ribbons, etc for embellishment
* scissors, pencil, ruler
* dressmaker's carbon paper
* freezer paper

STEP BY STEP

1 Trace or photocopy the heart template on page 95. Following the technique for working with dressmaker's carbon paper (see page 36), transfer all the lines of the design onto your foundation fabric (**a**). Go round this outline with a line of tacking stitches in a contrasting colour, then cut out the shape leaving a 2.5cm (1in) seam allowance (**b**).

2 Using the same method, copy the complete heart design onto freezer paper (**c**). Cut out the individual shapes 1-11 (**d**).

3 Decide which fabric you want to use for which patch; remember that the heart is small, so you don't want to use too many different colours, and pick fabrics that harmonise well.

4 Iron the numbered freezer paper shapes onto **the right sides** of your selected fabrics. Cut out the fabric pieces, adding a 2.5cm (1 inch) seam allowance on the outside edges (the ones marked III) and a 1cm (⅜in) seam allowance on all the other sides (**e**). On the edges marked *, turn the seam allowance to the back and press (**f**); these edges are the ones which overlap the neighbouring patch or patches.

5 Pin piece 1 in position on the foundation fabric. With right sides facing up, add all the other pieces 2-11 in sequence by pushing them under each other or – in the case of patches 10 and 11 – by appliquéing or slipstitching. You should end up with an overlap over the heart outline formed by the seam allowance (**g**).

6 Iron the whole heart shape, then embroider over the seams and some of the patches (**h**) as you wish, using a mixture of embroidery stitches, shisha, beads etc.

TIP: By ironing the crazy patchwork before you embroider it, you avoid flattening your embellishments.

7 Lay the front of the cushion over the backing fabric, right sides together, and pin; machine stitch all round the tacked line, leaving an opening at the top for turning (**i**). (If you're using a length of ribbon to hang the cushion, stitch this into the seam on each side of the opening at this stage.)

8 Finally, turn the heart right side out and stuff it with the polyester filling (and pot pourri or lavender if you're using it). Slipstitch the opening closed (**j**).

Crazy Patchwork Cushion

The idea of using freezer paper for crazy patchwork came about as the result of losing a cushion! I'd been commissioned to make a patchwork cushion, but it was lost in transit, so I had to make another one – an exact copy of the first. Copying the pattern wasn't difficult, but the fabrics – or rather the lack of them – did present a problem. I only had the remnants of the fabrics I'd used for the original cushion; not nearly enough to use the usual, fairly wasteful, way of cutting patches for crazy patchwork.

To make the best use of the bits of fabric I did have, I cut pieces of paper to the shapes of the patches and tried to pin these on the various remnants. But I quickly ran into trouble: I was working with velvets, brocades and laces, and the velvets moved each time I put a pin in. And the brocades and laces weren't much easier to handle.

I'd always used freezer paper for appliqué, so I thought, why not try it for crazy patchwork? And it worked perfectly. I re-drew the pattern of the 'lost' cushion on freezer paper, numbered all the individual shapes, and marked where they butted up to each other. I also marked the outside edges. I then cut the freezer paper up into its numbered shapes, ironed the pieces onto the right sides of the fabric remnants, cut out the shapes, and stitched them onto the foundation fabric. I never looked back!

Finished size: 35cm (14in) square

YOU WILL NEED:
* foundation fabric 40cm (16in) square
* fabric for the back of the cushion 40cm (16in) square

* cushion pad 35cm (14in) square
* large scraps of various opulent fabrics (eg silk, sateen, brocade, lace) for the crazy patches – you'll need perhaps 7 or 8 different colours and textures
* a few scraps of fabric in toning colours and a surprise piece (eg metallic, or silk tissue, or a crunched fabric) to make your cushion 'sing'
* matching sewing thread
* embroidery thread
* beads, sequins and mirrors for embellishment
* 165cm (65in) cord or braid for piping the edges
* scissors, pencil, ruler
* tracing paper and dressmaker's carbon paper
* freezer paper

STEP BY STEP

1 Photocopy the cushion template on pages 96-97, enlarging it by 133%. Following the technique for working with dressmaker's carbon paper (see page 36), transfer the design onto your foundation fabric (**a**). Go round this outline with a line of tacking stitches in a contrasting colour, then cut out the shape leaving a 2.5cm (1in) seam allowance (**b**).

2 Use the same method to copy the design on to the freezer paper (**c**).

3 Now choose which fabrics you'd like for which part of the design. Once you've decided, cut the freezer paper up into its individual numbered shapes (**d**); you can do this in sections to make it easier to handle.

TIP: If you cut tiny scraps of fabric and place them on your design where you're thinking of using them, it will give you an idea of how the overall colour balance will work. You can move the scraps around on the design and see which combination works best.

4 Iron the numbered freezer paper shapes onto **the right sides** of your selected fabrics (**e**). Cut out the fabric pieces, adding a 2.5cm (1 inch) seam allowance on the outside edges (the ones marked III) and a 1cm (⅜in) seam allowance on all the other sides (**f**). On the edges marked *, turn the seam allowance to the back and press (**g**); these edges are the ones which overlap the neighbouring patch or patches.

5 Pin piece 1 in position on the foundation fabric. With right sides facing up, add all the other pieces 2 – 45 in sequence by pushing them under each other or by appliquéing or slipstitching. You should end up with an overlap over the cushion outline formed by the seam allowance (**h**).

6 Iron the cushion before you begin to add embellishments (once you embroider, you don't want to flatten the decoration). Now embroider over seams and some patches – see the stitch list on page 22 for various embroidery designs, and use beads and shisha if you wish (**i**).

7 When you're satisfied with all the embroidery, lay the front of the cushion over the backing fabric, right sides together, and pin. Machine stitch all round, leaving a 15cm (6in) opening for turning (**j**). Turn the work right side out, insert the cushion pad, then close the opening with small stitches. Slipstitch cord around the edge (**k**); begin and end at one corner, pushing the raw ends of the cord into the corner of the seam.

8 If you'd like some extra decoration, make four tassels for the corners of the cushion (**l**). Follow the instructions on page 33, using silk thread or a combination of cotton knitting yarn and metallic embroidery thread, and winding the yarns round a 13cm (5in) wide piece of card.

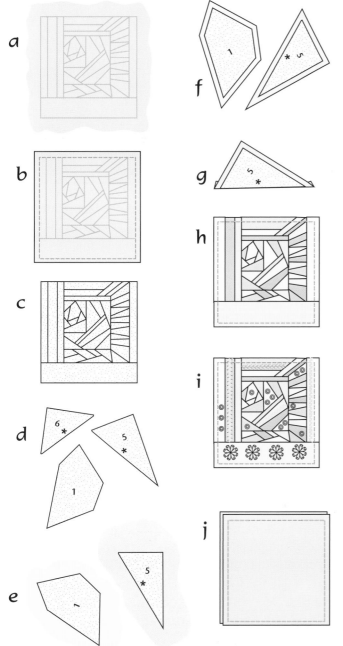

Beadwork Projects

Christmas Star or Pendant

Earlier in the book I've talked about beading onto fabric, and I've used that technique in many of the projects too. It's also possible, though, to use beads on their own, threaded together in different patterns to create free-hanging designs. This little five-pointed star, which you can use as a Christmas decoration or a pendant, is easy to make – you only need a few beads and bugles. Once you've seen how easy the star is, your success may encourage you to have a go at something more ambitious such as the larger star, or the hair ornament on page 66.

YOU WILL NEED:

FOR A SMALL STAR OR PENDANT

✴ 50 small beads

✴ 10 bugles

✴ strong thread (Nymo, or quilting thread) drawn through beeswax or thread conditioner

FOR A LARGE STAR OR PENDANT

✴ small beads

✴ bugles

✴ large bugles

✴ strong thread as above

a

b

c

d

e

f

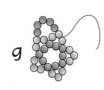

g

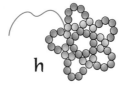

h

i

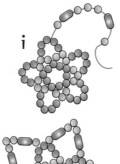

j

STEP BY STEP

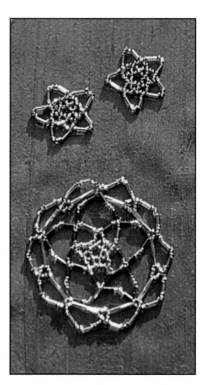

TO MAKE THE SMALL STAR

1 Thread a bead needle with at least 50cm (20in) of strong thread and pick up 10 small beads (**a**). Form these into a circle by taking the needle through all the beads again (**b**). (If you wish you can do this twice to strengthen the circle.)

2 Pick up three new beads on the needle to start the second row (**c**). From your position on the circle, leave a gap of one bead, then take the needle through the next bead; this forms a small point (or picot) of beads on the edge of the circle (**d**). Repeat this step four times (**e**), but on the fourth repeat go through the first bead of the circle again. To finish the second row, and to start the third, take the needle up through the first two beads of the first picot.

3 Pick up five new beads on the needle (**f**), go through the middle bead of the next picot and form a loop (**g**). Repeat this four more times so that you have five loops (**h**). Go through the first three beads of the first five-bead loop to start the next row.

4 Pick up one bead, one bugle, three beads, one bugle and one bead (**i**). Go through the third bead of the previous row to form a loop, and repeat this four times (**j**); finish the row by going up through the first bead, then the bugle and 2 beads.

5 Fasten off the thread by going through the last bead and looping it into a knot twice; cut off the thread.

TO MAKE THE LARGE STAR

1 Begin as described on page 64 for the small star, up to and including step 4.

2 Start row five by going up through the previous row to the centre of the point (that is, through two beads, one bugle and two beads again), as shown in **a**.

3 Pick up a sequence of one bugle, three beads, one bugle, one bead, one bugle, three beads and one bugle (**b**); take the needle through the middle bead of the previous row. Repeat this whole sequence four times (**c**). Take the needle through one bugle, three beads and one bugle into the centre bead (**d**), ready to start row six.

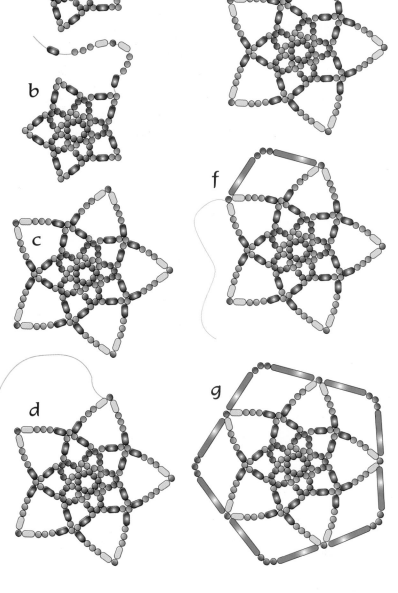

4 Pick up one large bugle (or two smaller ones), three beads, and one large bugle (or two smaller ones) as shown in **e**, and take the needle through the middle bead of the previous row (**f**). Repeat this sequence four times (**g**).

5 For the final row: pick up two beads, one bugle, three beads, one bugle, and two beads, and take the needle through the middle bead of the previous row. Repeat this sequence nine times so that you end up with ten loops (**h**). Finish off the thread by taking it through the final knot and tying a double knot; trim off the ends.

You can continue working circuits of loops to make very large circles, as the gold example (*above*) shows.

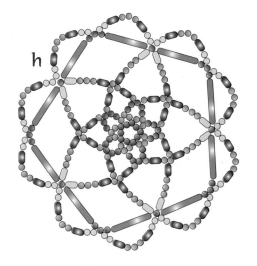

Hair Ornament or Snood

This highly decorative hair decoration is based on a head-dress I saw in Delhi on my last trip; it's reminiscent of the 1920s and the styles worn by the flappers. The beading is quite straightforward, and the finished item is a fun project for the young at heart to wear.

YOU WILL NEED:

✳ plenty of beads – at least 45-60g (1½ - 2oz) of round beads and the same of bugles, including 10g (⅓oz) of medium (3mm) beads

✳ a good 10yd/10m of thread

✳ straw needle for the fringe (an appliqué needle is fine for the other beading)

STEP BY STEP

1 Begin the crown of the snood as if you were making the large star on page 65; work the beading up to step 5, ending up with ten loops.

2 Start the next row (row 8) by taking the needle through the two beads, one bugle and two beads from the previous row. (Throughout this design you'll finish each row, and get ready to begin the next one, in the same way, by going into the picot of the previous row.) Pick up three beads, one bugle, five beads, one bugle and three beads on your needle (**a**); take the needle into the picot of the previous row to create a loop. Repeat this sequence nine times, each time going into the picot of the previous row (**b**).

3 For the next row, make a series of ten loops which this time each consist of five beads, one bugle, five beads, one bugle and five beads (**c**).

4 Now pick up three beads, one bugle and three beads, and take the needle through the middle of the five beads (that is, the third bead) of the previous row. Pick up the same sequence of beads and go through the picot of the last row; in this way you create two smaller loops outside each loop of the previous row (**d**). Continue this sequence all the way round the design so that you end up with 20 loops.

5 Continue making smaller loops in this way until you reach the required diameter; test this out by laying the bead net flat on the crown of the head.

6 Decrease the number of beads slightly to form a headband. Using only round beads (not bugles), make a series of chain loops, using an odd number of beads for each chain and always working into the middle of the previous chain (**e**). (Don't decrease the number of beads in the loops any more.)

TIP: It works well, and looks good, if you use a contrasting bead for the centre of

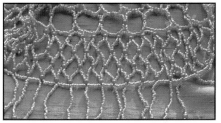

each chain, as I've done with the large bright pink beads in the sample above.

7 Now it's time to make a fringe for the front of the net. Thread the straw needle with a long, strong thread (drawn through beeswax); pick up, in order, about 20 beads, a medium (3mm) bead, and then three beads (**f**).

8 Take the needle back through one bead, then through the medium bead, up through the string of beads, and finally back through the head of the loop where you started. You now have the first thread of your fringe (**g**).

9 Pick up 10 beads on the needle, go through the next loop (**h**), and then follow steps 7 and 8 to make

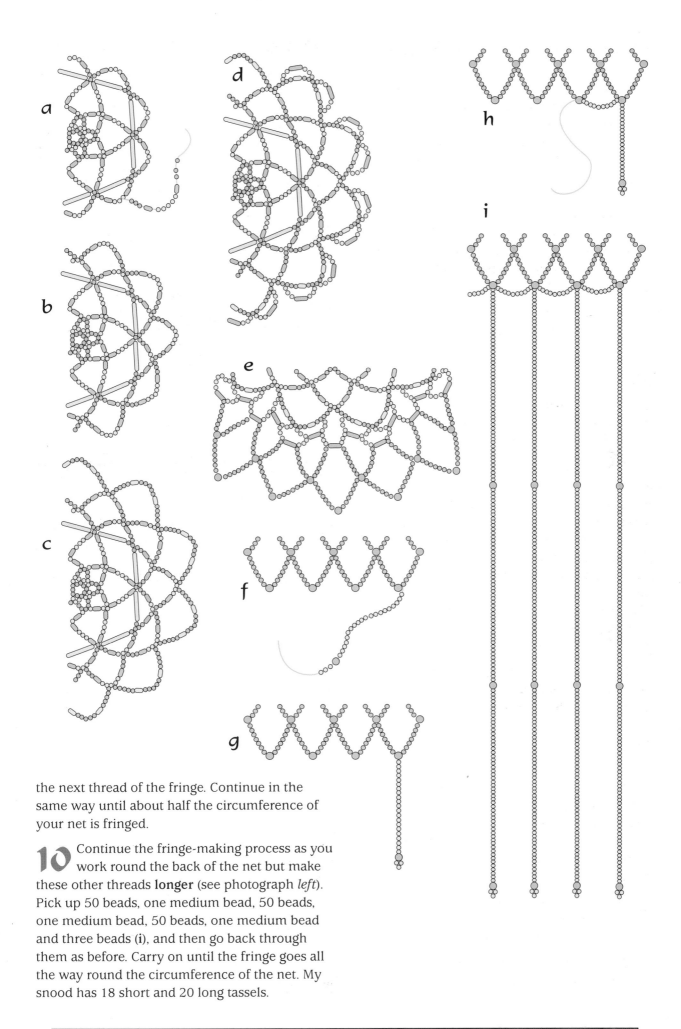

a

b

c

d

e

f

g

h

i

the next thread of the fringe. Continue in the same way until about half the circumference of your net is fringed.

10 Continue the fringe-making process as you work round the back of the net but make these other threads **longer** (see photograph *left*). Pick up 50 beads, one medium bead, 50 beads, one medium bead, 50 beads, one medium bead and three beads (**i**), and then go back through them as before. Carry on until the fringe goes all the way round the circumference of the net. My snood has 18 short and 20 long tassels.

Pillbox Hat

This pillbox hat was inspired by the hats or caps worn in Northern India by many men, especially Muslims. The hats are sometimes rather like skull-caps, perhaps plain or lacy in appearance, and sometimes more like the pillbox caps nineteenth-century soldiers wore in Britain. The pillbox hats are often richly decorated or embroidered.

The finished size of the hat shown here is 17.5cm (7in) in diameter, 9cm (3½in) in height, and 60cm (24in) circumference. If you need a larger or smaller hat, adjust the pattern pieces and the fabric requirements accordingly.

YOU WILL NEED:

* fabric for the crown of the hat, 20cm (8in) square

* lining for the crown, as above

* fabric for the sides of the hat, 11cm (4¼in) deep and 64cm (25in) long

* lining for the sides, as above

* 5g (⅙oz) of gold beads

* 10g (⅓oz) of purple beads

* 5g (⅙oz) of gold bugles

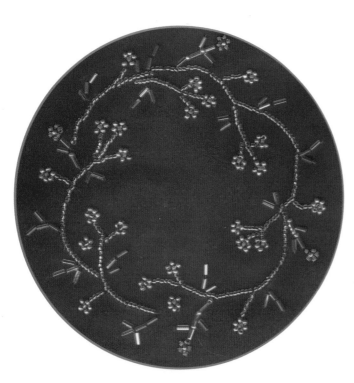

* strong thread (Nymo or silk drawn through beeswax, or quilting thread) in matching colours for beading

* sewing thread to match the hat fabric

* beading needle (No 11 or 12 appliqué or quilting needle)

* tracing paper and dressmaker's carbon paper (I used yellow carbon paper when I worked on purple velvet)

* a sharp, hard pencil for tracing

STEP BY STEP

1 Trace or photocopy the designs for the crown and sides of the hat on pages 98 and 99.

2 Draw or trace the circular outline of the crown on to your chosen fabric. Inside this circle, draw the bead design for the crown (**a**). The easiest way to do this is by using dressmaker's carbon paper (see page 36).

3 Using the same process, transfer the design for the side of the hat (page 99) to the fabric. The design measures 20cm (8in), so draw it **three times** to make a design 60cm (24in) long – the measurement of the side of the finished hat (**b**).

4 Now stitch the beads in place on the crown and the side. Using a strong matching thread and a thin needle, thread and attach all the beads singly (see page 31), following the lines of the designs (**c**).

5 Lay the beaded side strip and the lining strip right sides together and stitch a seam down one long side to join them (**d**). Open out (**e**), then with right sides still together, stitch the short ends of the lined strip together to form a circle (**f**), checking that the finished circuit matches the circumference of your circular crown section. Fold the strip so that the beaded design is on the outside and the lining inside (**g**).

6 Cut the crown shape out, leaving a generous seam allowance, then cut a matching circle from the lining fabric (**h**). Pin the two circles together, **wrong sides** facing, and attach the side strip to the crown by hand or machine (**i**), neatening the seam as required.

TIP: You can use the different beads in any combination that looks good; I've included (opposite) a close-up of my work in case you want to imitate the way I've used the beads. I've worked the main stem parts of the designs in tiny seed beads, with some of the flower stems and the offshoot stems in a mixture of bugle beads and slightly larger seed beads. Most of the flowers are created with a single purple bead in the centre surrounded by gold seed beads, but I've worked occasional ones the other way around for variety.

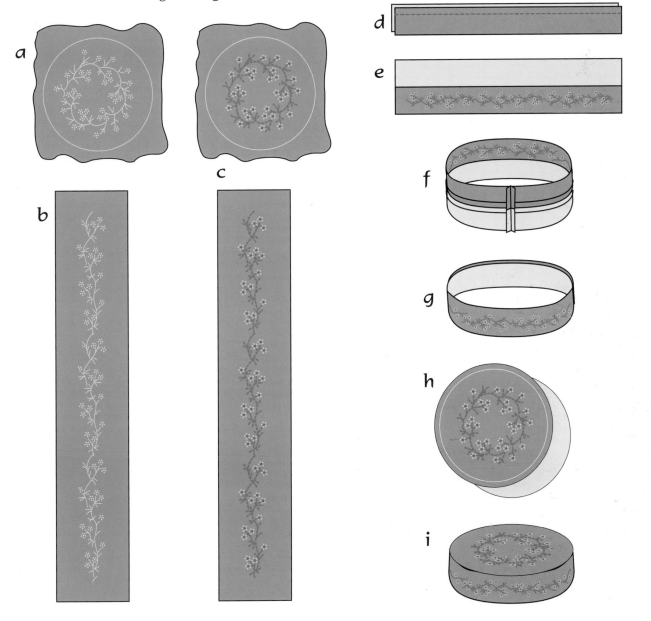

Beadwork with Bonding Web

I enjoy embroidering a single motif – perhaps a flower, or a paisley design – as a separate item and then appliquéing it onto another item; this technique works well on garments, quilts and cushions. By experimenting I've also found that, instead of making a separate motif using appliqué, I can achieve the same result using bonding web.

To use bonding web you need a firm foundation fabric the size of your intended shape plus an overlap of at least 5cm (2in) all round. You may well find that a small embroidery hoop is useful, too, for keeping the work flat while you stitch, and a small pair of sharp scissors, for close trimming, is a must. I've shown below two motifs that work well with bonding web, but you can also use the same technique for some of the other motifs in this book, as well as trying out your own designs.

YOU WILL NEED:

FOR A FLOWER

* 18 x 13cm (7 x 5in) foundation fabric
* six pearls and one bead for the centre of the flower, and quite a few purple sequins
* small blue-purple iridescent beads
* strong thread (Nymo, quilting thread or silk thread) strengthened by beeswax
* appliqué needle No 11 or 12
* small piece of bonding web

FOR A PAISLEY DESIGN

* foundation fabric in yellow/gold 25 x 15cm (10 x 6in)
* roughly 150 gold bugle beads
* approximately 30cm (12in) gold braid
* large curtain ring, 3cm (1¼in) across
* gold thread for couching and for covering the curtain ring
* large mirror, 3cm (1¼in) across
* small multicoloured beads to surround the mirror
* large bead, 1cm (⅜in) wide
* approximately 35 3mm beads
* strong matching thread (Nymo or quilting thread) strengthened by beeswax
* appliqué needle No 11 or 12
* small piece of bonding web, 15 x 10cm (6 x 4in)

STEP BY STEP

TO MAKE A FLOWER

1 Trace or photocopy the flower design on page 100 and use it as a template to cut a piece of foundation fabric, adding seam allowances all the way around. Mark the centre point and the five petal shapes on the fabric (**a**).

Use your needle to pick up the bead which will form the centre of the flower and stitch it onto the centre of the foundation fabric shape. Pick up and stitch the six pearls one by one, so that they surround the centre bead (**b**). Surround these pearls, in turn, with a row of closely-stitched sequins, positioned so that they overlap each other (**c**).

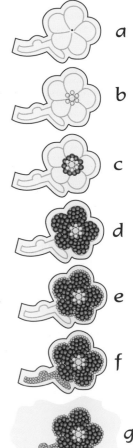

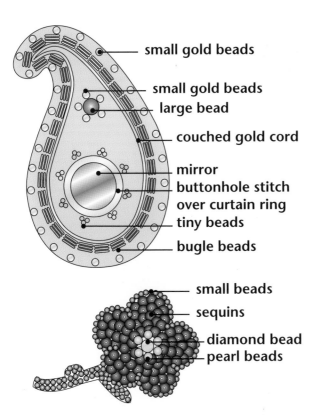

small gold beads

small gold beads

large bead

couched gold cord

mirror
buttonhole stitch
over curtain ring
tiny beads

bugle beads

small beads

sequins

diamond bead

pearl beads

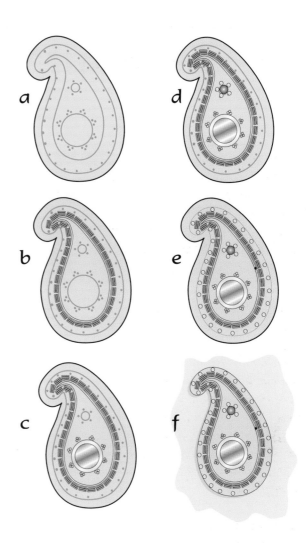

a

b

c

d

e

f

2 Fill in the five petal shapes with purple sequins (**d**); make sure that you stay within the pencilled lines. Outline the petals by surrounding them with the small iridescent beads, again picking them up and securing them one by one (**e**). Add two rows of beads to form the stem, leaf and bud (**f**).

3 Iron the bonding web onto the back of the foundation fabric (follow the maker's instructions carefully) and with fine, sharp scissors cut round the flower, stem, leaf and bud. Cut as closely to the embroidery as you can; the bonding web will prevent any fraying.

4 Leave the paper backing of the bonding web on until you're ready to attach the motif onto your chosen fabric; then peel off the paper and, with a cloth covering and protecting the embroidery, iron the embroidered flower on to the fabric (**g**).

TO MAKE A PAISLEY DESIGN

1 The method for creating the paisley design is essentially the same as for making the flower (above). Trace or photocopy the paisley design from page 100 and transfer it to the foundation fabric; cut out the shape, leaving a generous seam allowance all round (**a**). Outline the shape with a triple row of bugle beads, then inside this triple row, couch down gold braid (**b**).

2 Now stitch round the curtain ring, covering it with buttonhole stitch in gold. Place the mirror in position on the paisley shape and lay the covered ring on top; with gold thread, stitch the ring in place to secure the mirror. Add groups of three beads all round the ring (**c**).

TIP: As an alternative to covering your own mirror surround, firms such as Glitterati (see page 119) sell rings which are already covered with stitching; some of these have beads around the edges too.

3 Next, stitch the large bead in place, and surround it with five or six 3mm gold beads (**d**). Add a few more of the 3mm gold beads at the edge of the design, outside the three rows of bugle beads (**e**).

4 Protect the beadwork with a cloth while you iron the bonding web onto the back of the shape, then cut away the surplus foundation fabric. Your paisley motif is now ready to use (**f**).

Elephant Wall-Hanging

India is a land of festivals. Virtually every temple in every town and across the country has its festival, and in the accompanying processions the elephants claim centre stage. Decorated from head to foot and adorned with tassels and bells, they stride majestically forth, recalling India's magnificent past when Mughal and Rajput rulers had stables full of elephants for great state occasions and for military campaigns.

Hathi pols, or elephant gates, are still characteristic features of most principal entrances to royal complexes. Usually, stone elephants are positioned at either side of the gate with the trunks of the animals rising up and meeting to form an arch over the opening. Nowadays, the mighty real elephants are only seen in full regalia at festivals; then they provide an impression of power and majesty you'll never forget.

The embellished elephant shape in the centre of this wall-hanging can be appliquéd to a plain background (see above) or one made in crazy patchwork (see page 75); I'll describe the plain one first, and then explain how to do the patchwork background. The finished size of the panel is 60 x 45cm (24 x 19in).

TIP: The lamé thread comes in a skein of 12 strands; if you use two strands in the needle at a time for all the embroidery, you'll have enough for the whole design.

YOU WILL NEED:

FOR THE ELEPHANT

* loosely-woven foundation fabric, 45 x 40cm (18 x 16in)
* fabric for the elephant itself, 50cm (20in) square
* plain silk, approximately 40cm (15in) square, for the decorations
* plain velvet, 20 x 15cm (8 x 6in), for the saddle blanket, and the same amount of fabric for the lining
* a mixture of beads and pearls, roughly 2oz of each
* roughly 1m (40in) gold braid (I used medium #16 Kreinik metallic) for couching the paisley design onto the blanket
* 1m (40in) gold filigree to go round the pearls on the paisley design and on the trunk
* four 1cm mirrors with gold rims
* 20 small bells for the feet
* two gold tassels for the tail and ear
* scrap of white fabric for the tusks
* large scrap of pink fabric for the tongue and trunk
* small flower to act as the cap which the elephants customarily wear (optional)
* matching thread to attach all the above items

FOR THE TASSELS

* fabric of your own choice, at least 40 x 90cm (18 x 36in)

FOR THE PLAIN BACKGROUND

* exotic fabric which tones well with your elephant fabric, 70 x 55cm (28 x 22in)
* fabric for the backing, the same size

FOR THE CRAZY PATCHWORK BACKGROUND

* loosely-woven foundation fabric approximately 70 x 55cm (28 x 22in)
* fabric for the backing, the same size as your foundation piece
* fabric for crazy patches: assorted plain-coloured silks, brocades, necktie fabrics, velvets, all colour-related, approximately one square metre (1sq yd) in total
* silk thread for attaching patches to the foundation fabric.
* skein of Anchor lamé No 300 (or roughly 10m/10yd similar thread)
* 1oz beads of any type
* black marker pen and large piece of paper

TIP: *The amount of fabric specified for the elephant provides enough to make the ear in the same fabric; the ear is attached between the head ornament and the saddle blanket (see step 7).*

STEP BY STEP

MAKING THE ELEPHANT

1 Trace or photocopy the two parts of the elephant shape (template **A**) on page 102-103. (Just draw the outline of the elephant; the details on the design are to show you where the embroidery is worked, and where the appliquéd patches fit.) Trace or photocopy templates **B, C, D, E, F, G, H, I, J** and **K** on page 101.

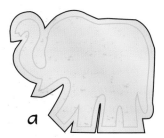

a

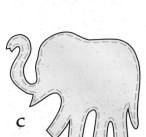

b

2 Cut out the elephant shape and pin it on top of your chosen elephant fabric; cut the shape out of the fabric, adding a generous seam allowance all round (**a**). Do exactly the same with the foundation fabric; you now have the elephant shape in your chosen fabric and on the foundation fabric (**b**).

c

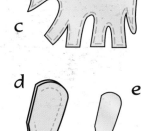

d   e

3 Place the first elephant shape over the one cut in foundation fabric, and use tacking stitches to sew the pieces together by turning the surplus fabric (ie, the seam allowance) to the back (**c**). To make it easier to fold the seam allowance under, clip both fabrics at the trunk, mouth, leg and tail areas.

4 For the ear, use template B to cut one shape right way round and one in reverse, adding seam allowances. Put the pieces right sides together and stitch a seam, leaving the long straight edge open for turning (**d**). Turn the ear shape the right way out (**e**).

5 Lay the saddle blanket fabric right side up on a flat surface, then position your lining fabric on top, right sides together. Mark the exact size of the saddle blanket and sew round the two long sides and one short side, leaving one short side open for turning (**f**). Turn the shape right side out, slipstitch the opening closed, embellish the blanket with closed herringbone stitch on all three sides, and add a fringe of beads (**g**).

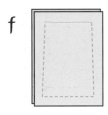

6 Outline the paisley pattern by couching the piece of metallic gold onto the centre of the velvet. Add pearls, and surround them with filigree wire in lazy daisy stitch (see page 23). (The wires are hollow – you thread a needle through them.) Embroider a flower design in the centre of the paisley shape (**h**), then attach the finished saddle blanket to the elephant (**i**).

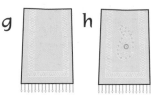

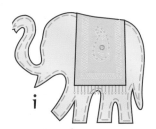

7 Use the other templates to cut patches from your chosen fabrics, adding a 5mm (¼in) seam allowance around each edge on all the pieces (**j**). Turn the seam allowances under on each patch and appliqué or slipstitch all the pieces to the elephant shape (**k**), trapping the raw edge of the ear underneath the head ornaments so that the ear flaps free of the body.

9 Cut two tusks from the white or cream fabric, and attach and embroider them as indicated, then appliqué or slipstitch the elephant to the centre of the background fabric (**m**).

10 Put the backing fabric and the elephant design right sides together, and stitch by hand or machine around the edges, leaving an opening for turning. Turn to the right side, and close up the opening with small stitches. Add a 5-7.5cm (2-3in) sleeve at the back for hanging.

8 Embroider the design with beads and closed-up herringbone stitch as indicated on the main template. Add the earring, bells, bead tassels and mirrors. Embroider the eye and, using the small piece of orange or pink fabric, add little shaped patches to indicate the mouth and the end of the trunk (**l**).

THE TASSELS

1 Cut the tassel fabric into strips 6mm (¼in) wide and 55mm (2¼in) long. Make little bundles of 25 strips and turn them into tassels (see pages 33-34). You need 60 small tassels to go all round the four sides of the hanging; sew each one into the edge of the hanging with a few firm stitches (**n**).

TO CREATE A CRAZY PATCHWORK BACKGROUND

1 On a piece of paper, mark a rectangle 70 x 55cm (28 x 22in); place the elephant template in the centre of the rectangle and draw round it (**a**). Using a pencil and ruler, draw random patches across the background area as shown in **b**; you don't need to copy the position of these lines exactly, but the diagram gives the general idea. Go over all the lines of the crazy pattern and elephant to get a really strong, clear outline, and then tape it to a flat surface. Now tape your foundation fabric over the drawing, right side up; with a sharp, hard pencil, trace the whole design onto the foundation fabric (**c**).

2 Cut up the drawing and use the pieces as templates to cut patches from your fabrics, adding about 13mm (½in) seam allowance all the way around each patch; remember to use the templates right side up on the right side of the fabrics. Pin patch 1 onto the foundation fabric. Follow the instructions for crazy patchwork (see page 20) to add all the other patches in turn until the whole background (minus the elephant shape!) is covered (**d**).

TIP: If you come across an angle where you can't stitch and flip the patch over in the usual way, you'll need to slipstitch your patches together

3 Work decorative embroidery over all the seams, and add a few beads for sparkle. Appliqué your finished elephant shape to the crazy patchwork background (**e**), then make up the wall-hanging as described on page 74 and finish it off with tassels as shown at the top of this page.

Embroidered Animal Mural

This hanging is inspired by murals seen in India – mainly from the Shekawati area – dating back to the eighteenth century; one of them can be seen in the photograph on page 77. The elephant represents strength, the horse is for power, and the camel is for love. For the main project I've stitched all the animals on one piece of background fabric to create a long mural; if you prefer to do just one of the animals, or to create a set of three separate panels, follow the guidelines in the tip at the bottom of page 78.

YOU WILL NEED:

FOR THE BACKGROUND
* fabric suitable for the whole embroidery, 50 x 30cm (20 x 12in)
* pencil, ruler and large piece of paper

FOR THE ANIMAL BODIES
* skein of black (or any dark colour) stranded cotton for the outlines, the border, and the horse's tail and mane
* skein of elephant-grey stranded cotton
* skein of mottled black/white stranded cotton for the horse
* skein of camel-coloured stranded cotton
* thin card for making templates

FOR EMBELLISHING
* half a skein of golden yellow stranded cotton for the elephant, and part of the horse's saddle and mane
* half a skein of blue/green stranded cotton for the border of the elephant's saddle and the peacock
* half a skein of blue stranded cotton for the camel's saddle
* skein of Anchor gold lamé for bracelets, necklaces and some outlines of the animals, and for the borders
* skein of variegated embroidery thread for the plant stems and leaves in the border
* packet of pearly beads for the centres of the bead flowers
* packet of small beads for the petals of the flowers
* embroidery needle suitable for your chosen thread
* beading needle (I use appliqué needle No 11 or 12)
* embroidery hoop (optional)

TIP: If you prefer, you could use space-dyed silk threads for the embroidery instead of stranded cottons.

STEP BY STEP

1 On your piece of paper, draw a rectangle 46 x 23cm (18 x 9in). Draw a second rectangle 2.5cm (1in) inside the first, to create a border shape (**a**). For the large mural, use the border design on pages 104-105 in two halves, splitting it where shown on the template. Trace the left-hand side of the design onto the left-hand side of the border, and the right-hand side of the design onto the right-hand side of the border (**b**).

TIP: If you have access to a photocopier, you can photocopy the border design and paste the two halves into your border shape for step 1.

2 Join up the stem lines with two wiggly lines, and add leaf and flower shapes to complete the border design (**c**). Using dressmaker's carbon paper (see page 36), transfer the whole of this border design to the background fabric (**d**).

3 Trace or photocopy the animal shapes on pages 104-106; you only need to draw the main outlines at this stage. Stick the shapes to cardboard and cut them out to create templates. Arrange the templates inside the border on the background fabric, and draw round their outlines with strong clear lines (**e**).

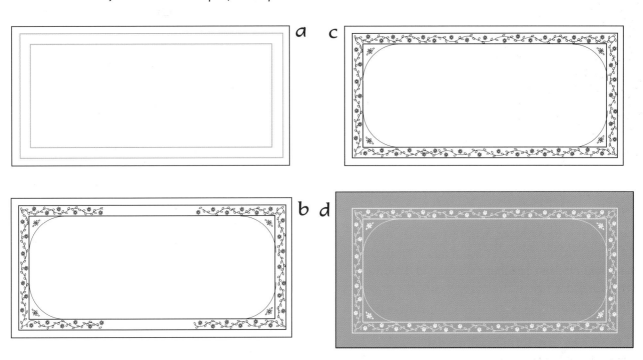

Decorative designs like this one inspired my stitched animal mural

4 Beginning and ending at the tip of the tail on each animal, stitch round the outlines in chain stitch (see page 23), using a dark colour. Then follow the **black** lines on the animal shapes to draw in all the other main lines (the various saddles and headgear); work chain stitch along all these lines, using the same thread (**f**).

5 Now you can begin to fill in the bodies. Use spirals and continuous lines of chain stitch – whatever shape best suits the section you're filling in. For the legs, work lines of chain stitch up and down the shapes. Cover all the different sections of the animals with chain stitch (**g**) before you begin the embellishment.

6 Working **over** the chain stitch, and following the guidelines on the animal drawings, embellish the designs with straight stitch (see page 26), lazy daisy stitch (see page 23), and beading (see pages 31-32). The photographs (pages 76 and 79) show some of the ways I've used embroidery and beading, but of course you can use your own choice of stitches and designs.

7 For the straight edges of the border, inside and outside, work a row of black (or dark) stem stitch then another row in gold. Follow the meanderings of the daisy chain: the main line of the stem is worked in chain stitch, the leaves are single lazy daisy stitches, and the little flowers are formed with small pearly beads – one medium-sized one surrounded by six smaller ones (**h**).

8 Outline the corner shapes with dark chain stitch, then fill them with chain stitch in variegated thread; decorate each one with a beaded flower-and-leaf motif (**i**). Add some short lines of stem stitch in green to suggest tufts of grass; finish off the fabric by hemming it all the way around, or mount the panel in a frame as a picture.

TIP: *You can, of course, make a hanging with just one of the animals, following the same method. I've embroidered each of the animals as an individual panel (see right); for these versions, use the border on pages 104-105 as it is, without splitting it.*

e

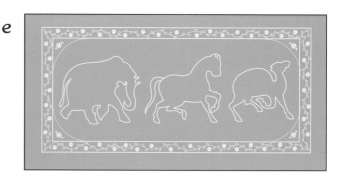

f

g

h

i

*Use beadwork and embroidery to embellish the designs in any way that works well;
try the ideas I've used on my panels, or try out your own ideas for borders
and embellishments*

Country Concerto

At first sight this small quilt/wall-hanging probably looks rather complicated, but have a look at how I constructed it, because you can then see how a seemingly difficult piece of work is actually built up from a few basic blocks or units. The individual pieces of stitching are not particularly challenging, but once lots of these individual pieces are assembled into a larger project, and

embellished with embroidery and beading, they produce a spectacular piece of needlework. The full finished wall-hanging as shown here measures 110cm (roughly 43in) square. It's made up of sixteen 25cm (10in) squares, surrounded by a 5cm (2in) border, but of course you don't have to use the whole design. You could, for example, work only the centre four panels, perhaps surrounded by a border, making an attractive small wall-hanging – or you could arrange the other 12 squares in three rows of four, or settle for a square hanging of three by three panels. The choice is yours! But note, no quilting is involved. The three layers (crazy patchwork, foundation fabric and backing) are held together by ties (see page 37). You can also simply use one or two of the embroidered motifs (featured on pages 107-110) and work them as greetings cards (see pages 51-54).

The centre four squares, with the rays radiating from the aubergine circle at the very centre of the hanging, are based on a traditional 19th century design, and my choice of colours for the rays attempts to take account of the colours of the time. But to decorate the circle, and for the four aubergine corner triangles, I chose intricate modern designs embroidered in stem stitch, then trapuntoed and beaded, and surrounded by kantha stitches.

If you look at the four centre squares, you'll see that each of them is divided into 16 rays (see the template on page 112). I used dupion as the principal fabric throughout, and the colours I chose were: aubergine, claret, antique pink, midnight, Tudor red, ivy, forest, chocolate, mocha, purple, blue, black, cream, leaf, dark green and rose. All of these came from 'Silk Theme Packs' from The Silk Route (see page 119). I used the same colours for the remaining twelve squares to ensure a basic unity, but as well as dupion I used the occasional lace, velvet, brocade and hand-marbled silk.

Throughout the piece the embroidery is worked in space-dyed fine silk to create the impression of old-fashioned workmanship, and uses closed herringbone stitch (see page 25) over the seams of adjoining squares and over the seams at the border. The embroidery on the border (see page 83) is my own design, but has strong

Indian influences. One last point on the embellishment. I used Indian embroidery motifs for the flowers, little elephants and peacocks, but I also brought in the countryside with Indian farmyard creatures (which are much as you'd find in Britain – piglets, ducks and other birds). I added a couple of cats, too, although I must say that in all my travels in India I've never seen a single cat (tigers excepted!). The stitches are all simple, such as herringbone and stem stitch (see page 25), and chain stitch and lazy daisy (see page 23).

The materials lists below show everything you'll need to create the full 16-panel hanging measuring 110cm (43in) square; for smaller projects adjust the requirements accordingly.

YOU WILL NEED:

FOR THE PATCHWORK

✳ foundation fabric 180 x 112cm (72 x 44in), which is enough for sixteen 30cm (12in) squares (finished size 25cm/10in square) and for the border

✳ three or four packs of silk pieces in themed colours

✳ bits of silk velvet, lace, ikat, etc for the crazy patchwork

✳ one fat quarter in aubergine (for the circle at the centre of the quilt, for the four triangles, and for the rouleau that finishes off the hanging)

✳ 5m (6yd) of narrow cord for the rouleau

- 36 x 112cm (14 x 44in) of antique rose fabric for the border
- 120cm (47in) square of fabric for the backing
- matching thread
- sewing needle, sharp No 10
- dressmaker's carbon paper.
- two pieces of freezer paper each 25cm (12in) square

FOR THE EMBROIDERY
- approximately five skeins of space-dyed fine silk thread
- some silk ribbon
- small buttons for flower-heads, plus a few other buttons
- antique beads, sequins and bugle beads
- pearls
- delica beads, copper-coloured
- diamonds for the centre beads in the border
- small scissors
- crewel embroidery needle No 9 or 8
- appliqué needle No 11 or 12 for beading

STEP BY STEP

1 From your foundation fabric cut:
sixteen patches each 30cm (12in) square
three borders each 110 x 6.5cm (44in x 2¾in)
one border 114 x 6.5cm (45½in x 2¾).

2 Photocopy the design for the central squares (see page 112), enlarging it to the correct size. Using dressmaker's carbon paper (see page 36), transfer the design to four squares of foundation fabric and to one piece of freezer paper. Cut the freezer paper into its constituent shapes. The asterisk (*) on the template design indicates where you have to fold the fabric over and where the edge of the fabric is coming over the next patch.

3 Iron the numbered freezer paper shapes on top of your selected fabrics. Cut out the fabric pieces, adding 1cm (⅜in) seam allowance all the way around; turn under the seam allowances on the seam lines marked * and press them.

4 Pin piece number 1 in position on the foundation fabric. Following the instructions for crazy patchwork with freezer paper (see page 21), add all the other pieces 2-16 in sequence by pushing them under each other or by slip stitching (a).

5 Peel the freezer paper shapes off the fabric, then re-use the shapes to repeat the process a further three times so that you finish up with the fan design on the four centre squares (b).

6 Cut the quarter-circle centre pieces, and the four triangular cornerpieces, from the aubergine fabric. (I preferred to have a seamless circle in the centre, so I drew a circle with a radius of 10cm/4in onto the aubergine fabric, and then cut it out with a 2cm/¾in seam allowance). If you're using four separate centre pieces, join them into a circle.

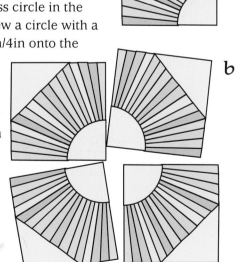

7 Trace or transfer the central and cornerpiece embroidery designs (see page 111) onto the centre piece(s) and the four triangles, then embroider the designs with stem stitch. (I threaded the channels on the designs with trapunto wool, but this is optional.) Add these pieces to the squares with the fan designs, and join the squares; if you wish, embroider over all or some of the seams to decorate them (see detail *left*). This completes the centre of the quilt (**c**); you can now start the twelve outer squares

8 Begin with the top left-hand square of the panel. Copy the design on page 113 onto the second square of freezer paper, cut out the numbered shapes (1-16), and iron them onto the appropriate fabrics. Using the same crazy patchwork technique that you used for the first four squares, cut out the shapes in fabric and build up the patchwork square (**d**). Embroider over all seams, then choose some of the designs from pages 107-110; transfer them to the crazy patches, and embroider them in your choice of stitches (see the stitch list on page 22 for ideas).

c

d

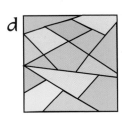

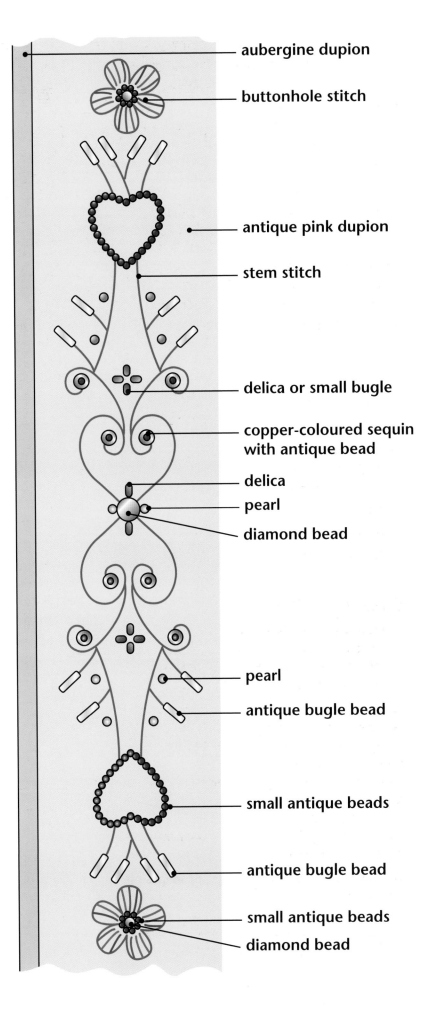

aubergine dupion

buttonhole stitch

antique pink dupion

stem stitch

delica or small bugle

copper-coloured sequin with antique bead

delica

pearl

diamond bead

pearl

antique bugle bead

small antique beads

antique bugle bead

small antique beads

diamond bead

9 Repeat the process in step 8 until you have enough complete squares to make up the full wall-hanging (**e**); join them as before, embroidering over the seams.

TIP: *You can use the same basic design for each of the crazy patchwork squares, varying them by using different colours and embroidery designs, or – better still – you can create your own crazy patchwork shapes so that no two squares are alike. It's a bit more work, but it's worth it!*

10 Now it's time for the border. Cut strips of silk to match the border strips you've cut from foundation fabric, and on each silk strip trace the border design shown on page 110 four times. (The border design is 25cm/10in long, the length of one square or panel, so it fits four times into each strip.) Tack the marked silk strips onto the corresponding strips of foundation fabric. Then, with a single strand and in stem stitch, outline the design and embroider it with beads; I've detailed the stitches I've used on the diagram on page 83. Add the border pieces to the patchwork panel.

11 Lay the backing fabric flat on the floor, wrong side up. Position the crazy patchwork on top, right side up, and pin the layers together. Turn the whole piece over so that the backing fabric is facing you and and tie the hanging at 10cm (4in) intervals (see page 37).

e

12 Cut whatever is left of the aubergine silk fat quarter into bias strips roughly 4cm (1½in) wide; join these and use them to make a rouleau, and thread the rouleau with the thin cord. Slipstitch the rouleau all round the outer edges of the hanging. Attach a 10cm (4in) sleeve to the back of the quilt for hanging.

TIP: *A clever little tool, the rouleau loop, is available from haberdasheries and is used for turning long, thin tubes of fabric. It's invaluable for making really professional-looking loops and ties.*

Indian Pictures

This 'memory quilt' incorporates lots of different photographs, which I've transferred to fabric (see page 37) so that I can use them in a stitched project. I chose a range of photographs which remind me strongly of India, and selected Indian embroidery methods and techniques to complement the whole ensemble. I picked the colours on the embroidered strips and round the photographs because, for me, their muted hues represent the eternal India – I wanted to avoid harsh and vivid colours.

I've used a series of small pictures built into squares or rectangles with a kind of foundation-pieced log cabin; these shapes in turn are both joined and separated by strips of embroidered, beaded and mirror-worked fabric. The whole panel is finally bordered by a richly-embroidered top band (with added beaten silver coins), and a lower edging of tassels.

The way I've constructed it, the finished central panel is 125cm (49in) from side to side and 75cm (29½in) deep. With its borders my finished piece measures 130 x 85cm (51 x 33½in). But once again, you don't have to create a whole large quilt; if you like the technique you can use it on just a few pictures, adding the spiral log cabin frames and then perhaps joining them with one or two small embroidered or beaded borders. Or you can use the borders on their own as ways of adding a touch of India to other projects. I'll describe each of the stages individually, so that you can mix and match them as you wish!

If you're thinking of making your own large memory quilt, you need to remember that there are three distinct stages in making a quilt or hanging like this:

- Transferring your chosen photographs onto fabric.

- Framing each photograph in turn, so that you have a number of square or rectangular panels.

- Linking the panels with strips of embroidered or patterned material to form the complete quilt or hanging. (You can then, if you wish, put a decorative border around the whole quilt.)

YOU WILL NEED:

FOR FRAMING THE PHOTOGRAPHS

✳ freezer paper

✳ hard, sharp pencil

✳ ruler;

✳ sharp paper scissors

✳ piece of foundation fabric for each photograph

✳ a selection of different-coloured fabrics (you'll find that quite small pieces are OK)

TIP: The pieces of foundation fabric must be larger than the finished size of the framed photograph: allow a generous 2cm (¾in) all round.

STEP BY STEP

TRANSFERRING THE PICTURES

1 Follow the instructions on page 37 to transfer your photographs to fabric.

FRAMING THE PICTURES

1 Trace or photocopy the design on page 114. (This design allows for standard-sized photographic prints (10 x 16cm/6 x 4in), but if your photographs are larger or smaller, adjust the size of the frame accordingly as you draw or photocopy. On page 115 I've included another template which will work in the same way for some smaller photographs.) The rectangular shape is the basic layout for your frame; trace it onto freezer paper, and onto the foundation fabric, making sure that you include the numbers as well as all the lines (**a**). (Keep the original drawing or photocopy so that you have a 'master' to which you can refer as you continue working.)

2 Take one piece of foundation fabric, lay it flat, position your fabric photograph at its centre, and pin it in place (**b**) – just a couple of pins will be enough.

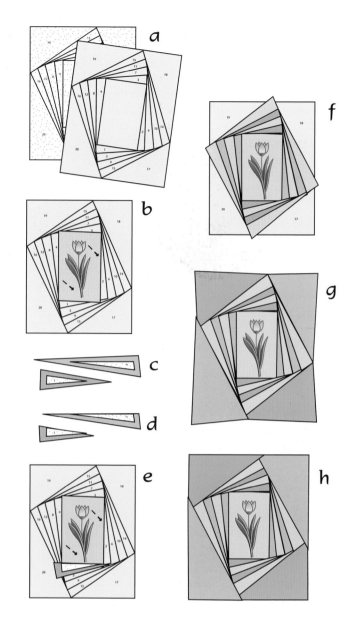

3 Take the freezer paper design and very carefully, using sharp scissors, cut out each of the twenty triangles. (You've already numbered each piece, so they won't get muddled up.) Once you have the twenty separate pieces of freezer paper you must match each one to a piece of fabric. Choose your colours and patterns carefully so that the finished panel is harmonious in colour, texture and pattern.

4 Iron the individual pieces of freezer paper (triangles 1-20) onto the **right sides** of the appropriate fabrics, and cut out each fabric shape, adding a seam allowance of 6mm (¼ in) all round (**c**). Turn under the seam allowances on all the edges marked with an asterisk (*), as shown in **d**.

5 Take triangle 1 and place the turned edge along the bottom edge of the photograph. Stretch and pin it firmly in place with a couple of pins, then slipstitch through the folded edge, the seam allowance of the photograph and the foundation fabric. The first triangle is now secured in position (e); remove the pins.

6 Use exactly the same technique to add triangle number 2, then continue in the same way adding pieces 3-16 in turn to create a frame (f). Always work anti-clockwise round the photograph.

7 Now fill the four corners by slipstitching pieces 17, 18, 19 and 20 in position. You now have your framed panel (g), with an untidy margin of material all round. Lay the panel flat and trim the excess fabric back to about 1cm (½in) all round (h); use a pencil and ruler to ensure straight edges – or, even better, a rotary cutter and ruler.

8 The final major step is to embroider and embellish the panel. Embroider over all the seams, using chain stitch, perhaps using beads and bugles to add variety of colour and texture.

9 Repeat the process for each photograph you want to frame.

JOINING THE PANELS

If you've created a series of framed pictures (perhaps all the same size or maybe a mixture of different-sized squares and rectangles), your next move is to join these panels to form the finished quilt or wall-hanging.

1 Lay the panels on a large flat surface and juggle them around until they create a pleasing combination of images and colours. If your panels are all the same size and shape you can simply join them with uniform strips of fabric (i). If they are different sizes and shapes (j), you'll be able to add rectangular strips of fabric to the edges until you've created a final square or rectangle (k). Choose whatever fabrics work well; the choice really is yours – plain or patterned fabrics, perhaps in a range of textures. When you're calculating the sizes you need for your strips, remember to add a generous seam allowance all round.

2 If you want to embroider or embellish the strips, do this before you attach them to the panels, because at this stage they are easier to hold and manipulate. You can create your own embroidery and beading patterns, or you can follow my ideas (see the templates on pages 116-117 and the stitching diagrams *overleaf*), adding beads or mirrors to taste. Don't forget that lovely and delicate designs can be achieved with quite simple stitches.

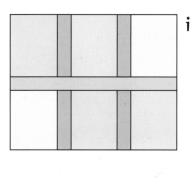

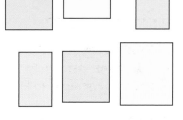

3 Slipstitch the strips to the appropriate panels until the top or surface of the quilt or wall-hanging is finished; embroider over all the seams if you wish.

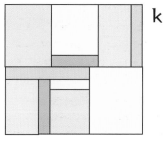

4 Your hanging isn't quite complete; it needs a backing, and perhaps a border. The best way of attaching the quilt top to the backing material is by tying (see page 37). Whether or not you add a border is very much a matter of personal choice; I like to have one as it defines the hanging and offers a lovely opportunity for imaginative decoration. Whatever you do, your memory quilt is bound to give a great deal of pleasure and revive lots of happy memories.

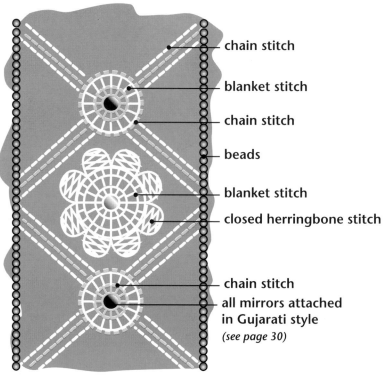

chain stitch

blanket stitch

chain stitch

beads

blanket stitch

closed herringbone stitch

chain stitch

all mirrors attached
in Gujarati style
(see page 30)

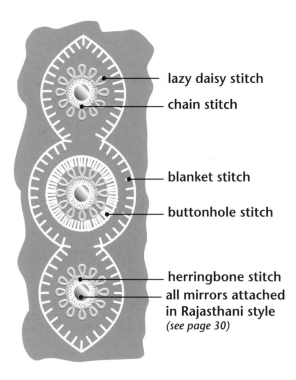

lazy daisy stitch

chain stitch

blanket stitch

buttonhole stitch

herringbone stitch

all mirrors attached
in Rajasthani style
(see page 30)

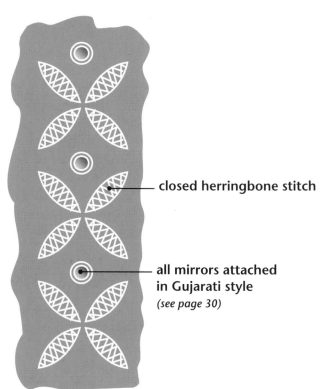

closed herringbone stitch

all mirrors attached
in Gujarati style
(see page 30)

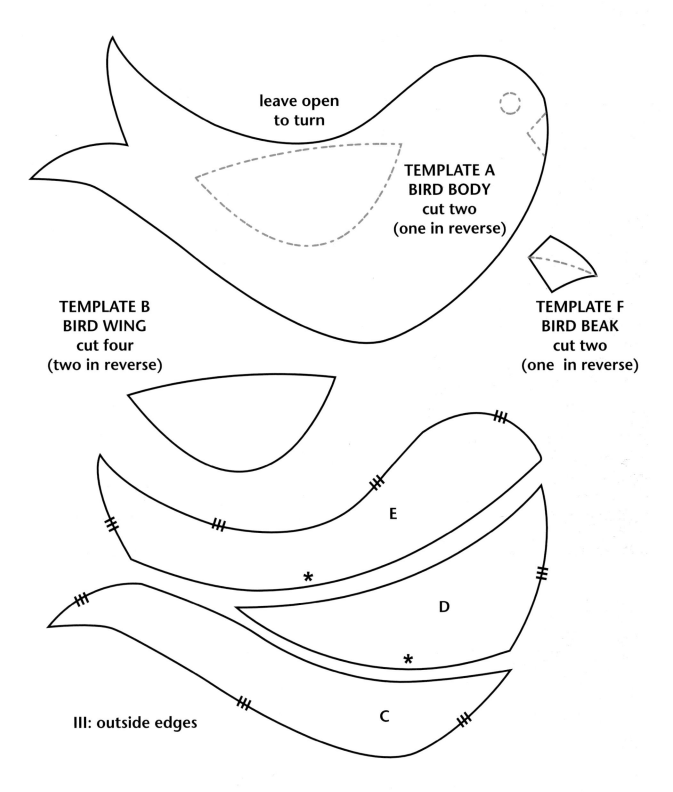

leave open
to turn

**TEMPLATE A
BIRD BODY
cut two
(one in reverse)**

**TEMPLATE B
BIRD WING
cut four
(two in reverse)**

**TEMPLATE F
BIRD BEAK
cut two
(one in reverse)**

E

*

D

*

C

III: outside edges

INDIAN BIRD ROPE
these templates are full size

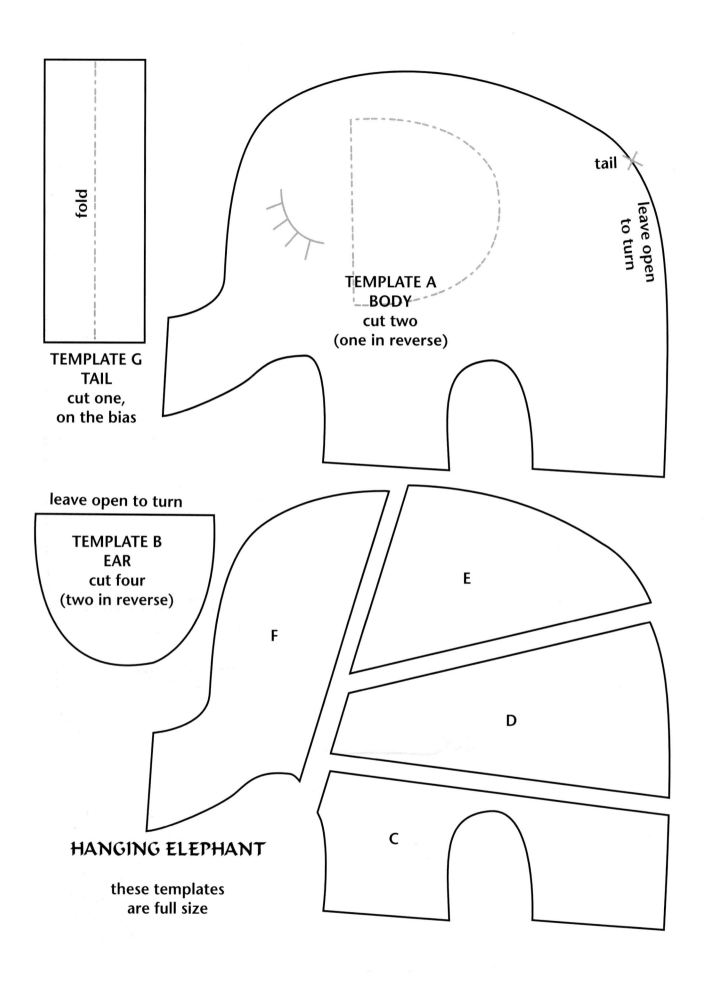

TEMPLATE G
TAIL
cut one,
on the bias

fold

TEMPLATE A
BODY
cut two
(one in reverse)

tail

leave open
to turn

leave open to turn

TEMPLATE B
EAR
cut four
(two in reverse)

E

F

D

C

HANGING ELEPHANT

these templates
are full size

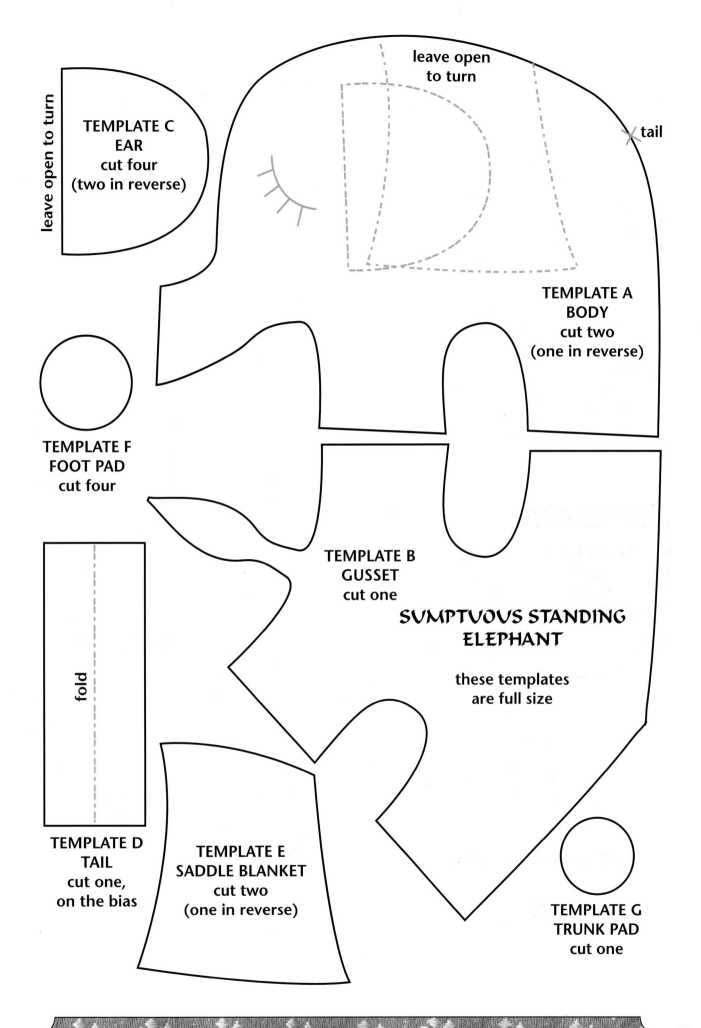

leave open
to turn

TEMPLATE C
EAR
cut four
(two in reverse)

leave open to turn

tail

TEMPLATE A
BODY
cut two
(one in reverse)

TEMPLATE F
FOOT PAD
cut four

TEMPLATE B
GUSSET
cut one

SUMPTUOUS STANDING
ELEPHANT

these templates
are full size

fold

TEMPLATE D
TAIL
cut one,
on the bias

TEMPLATE E
SADDLE BLANKET
cut two
(one in reverse)

TEMPLATE G
TRUNK PAD
cut one

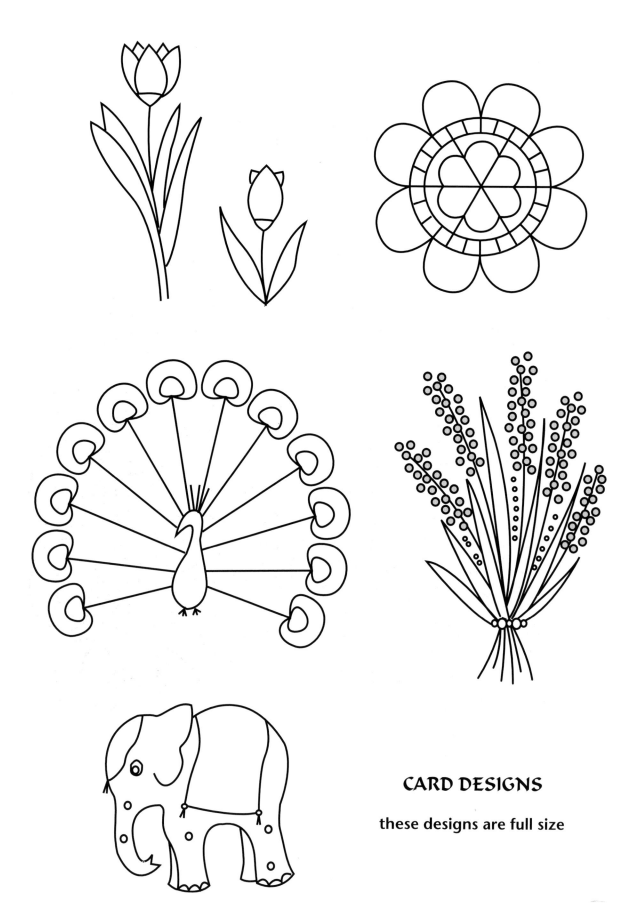

CARD DESIGNS

these designs are full size

PEACOCK EVENING BAG
embroidery motif

this design is full size

CHAIN STITCH SAMPLER
enlarge by 141% (A4 to A3),
to 25cm (10in) square

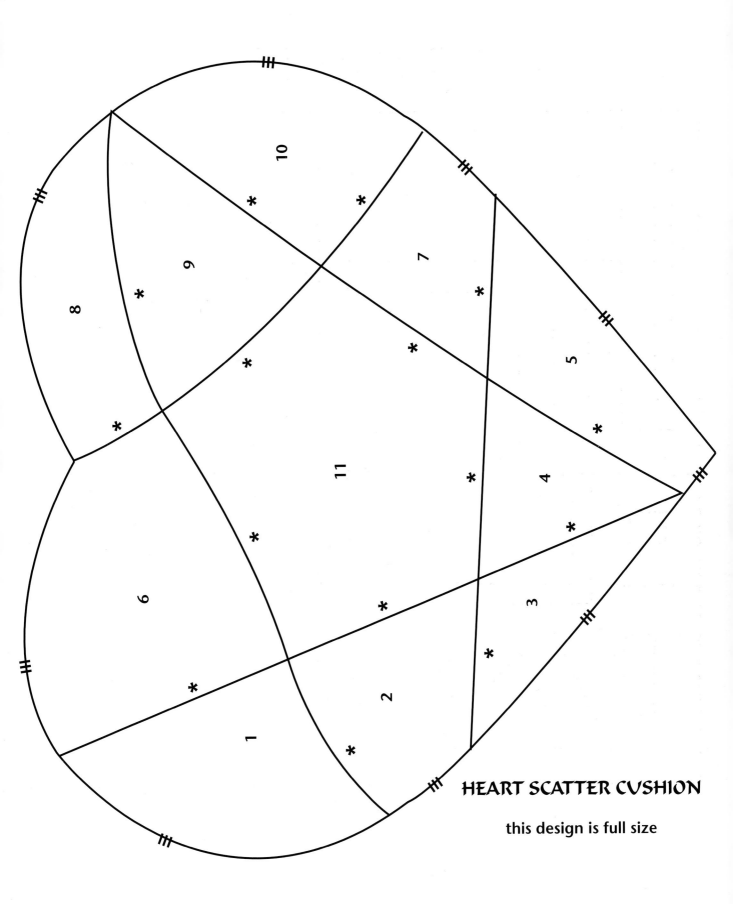

HEART SCATTER CUSHION

this design is full size

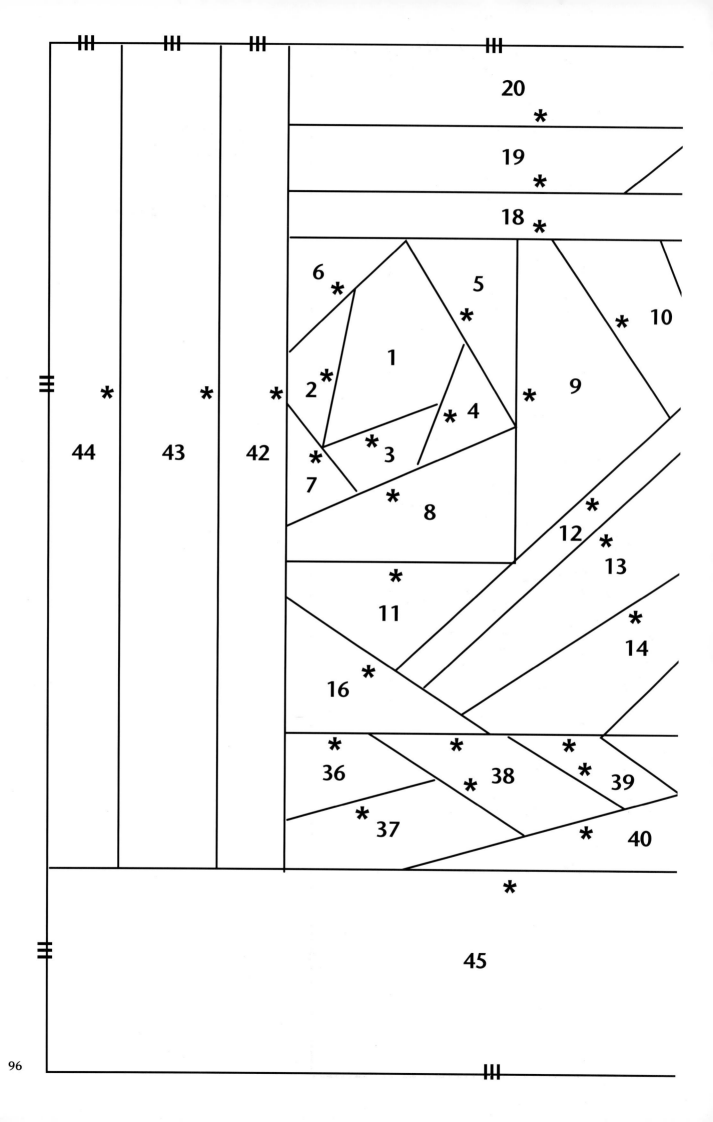

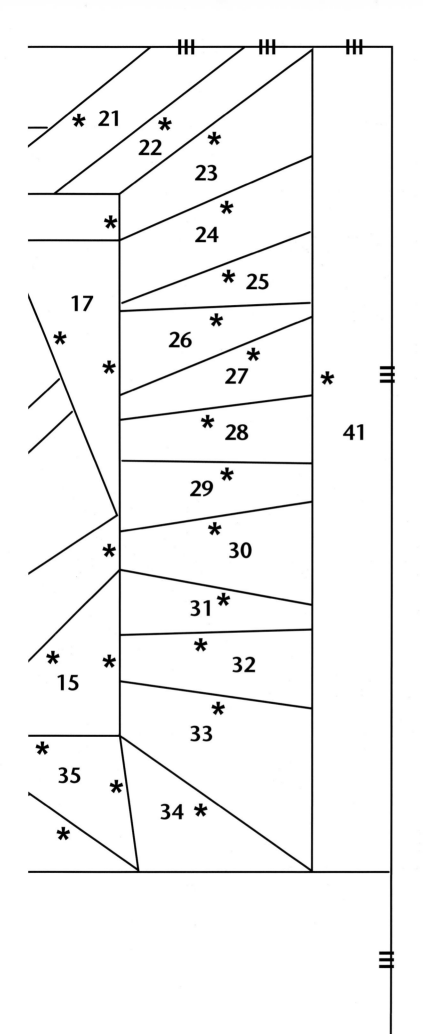

CRAZY PATCHWORK CUSHION

enlarge by 133%,
to 36cm (14in) square

PILLBOX HAT
CROWN
template A

this design is full size

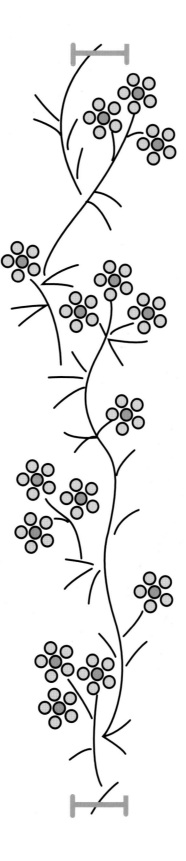

PILLBOX HAT
SIDE
template B

draw the section
between the repeat marks

three times
this design is full size

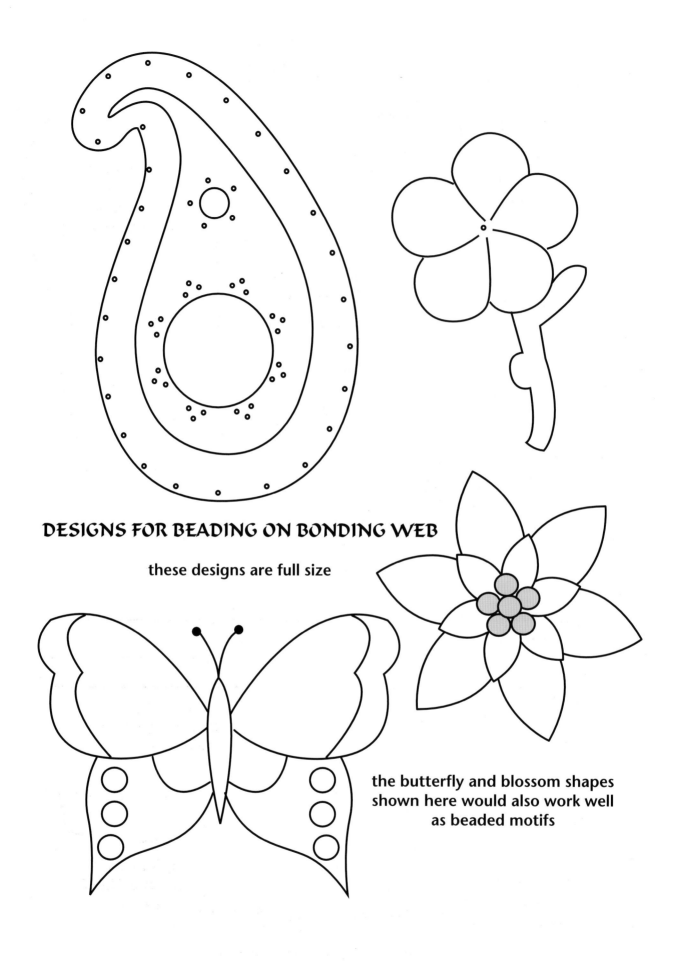

DESIGNS FOR BEADING ON BONDING WEB

these designs are full size

the butterfly and blossom shapes
shown here would also work well
as beaded motifs

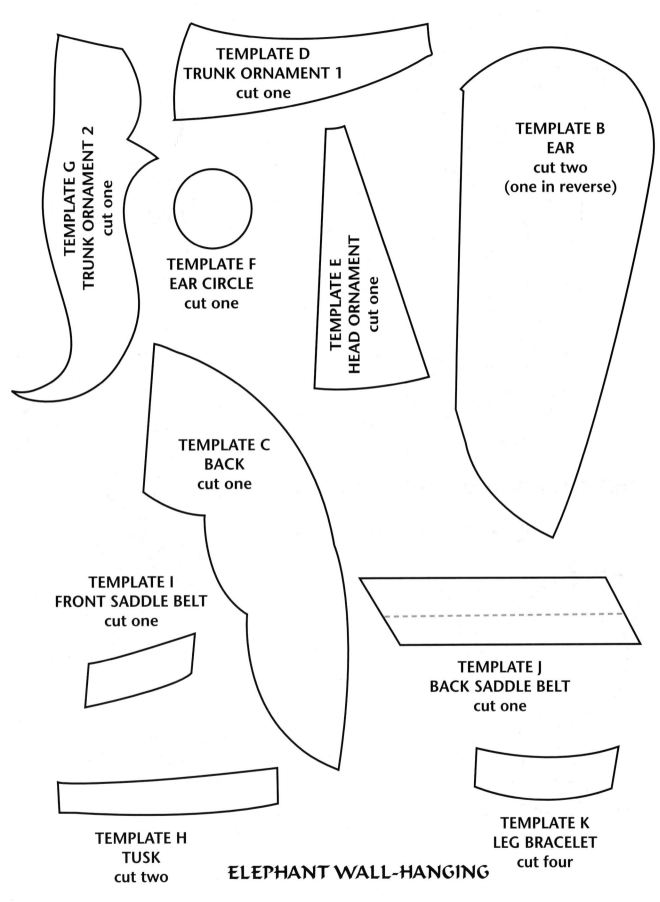

TEMPLATE D
TRUNK ORNAMENT 1
cut one

TEMPLATE G
TRUNK ORNAMENT 2
cut one

TEMPLATE B
EAR
cut two
(one in reverse)

TEMPLATE F
EAR CIRCLE
cut one

TEMPLATE E
HEAD ORNAMENT
cut one

TEMPLATE C
BACK
cut one

TEMPLATE I
FRONT SADDLE BELT
cut one

TEMPLATE J
BACK SADDLE BELT
cut one

TEMPLATE H
TUSK
cut two

TEMPLATE K
LEG BRACELET
cut four

ELEPHANT WALL-HANGING

these templates are full size

ELEPHANT WALL-HANGING
TEMPLATE A
BODY
cut two
(one in foundation fabric)

this design is full size

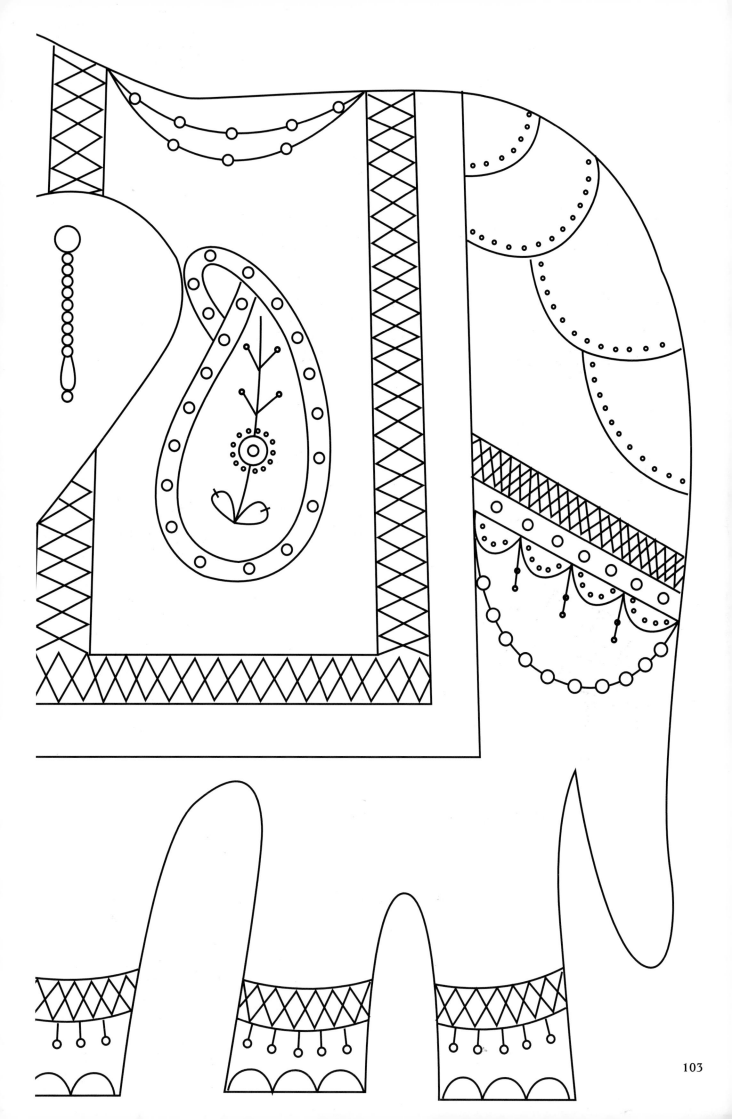

for the large mural,
split the border design
at the points shown

ANIMAL MURAL
elephant and border

these designs are full size

ANIMAL MURAL
camel and horse

these designs are full size

COUNTRY CONCERTO
embroidery motifs

these designs are full size

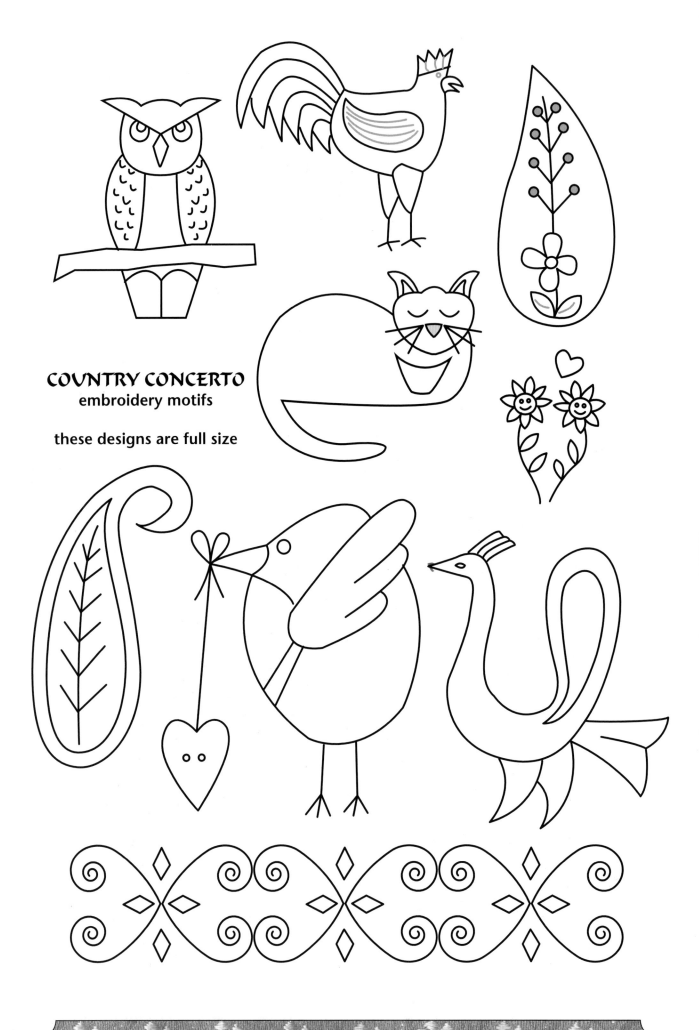

COUNTRY CONCERTO
embroidery motifs

these designs are full size

COUNTRY CONCERTO
embroidery motifs

these designs are full size

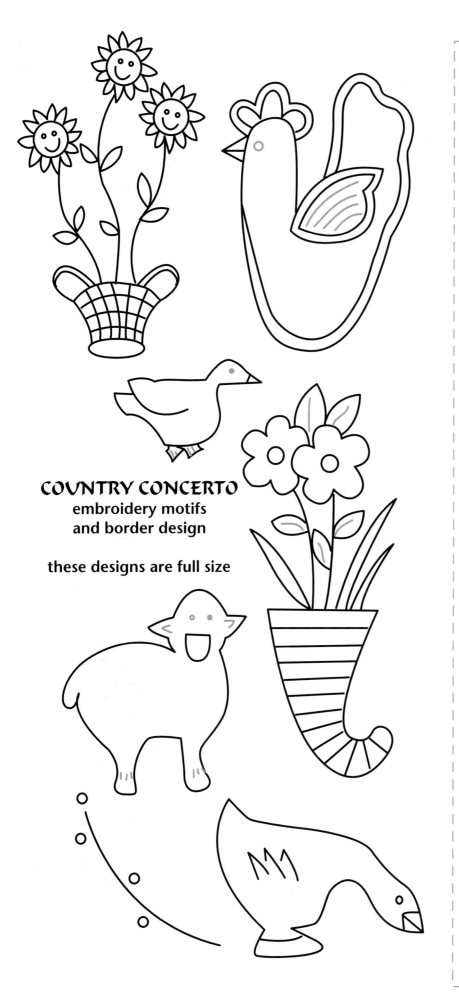

COUNTRY CONCERTO
embroidery motifs and border design

these designs are full size

COUNTRY CONCERTO
motifs for the central circle
and the cornerpieces

these designs are full size

COUNTRY CONCERTO
plan 1

enlarge this design by 136%, to 25cm (10in) square

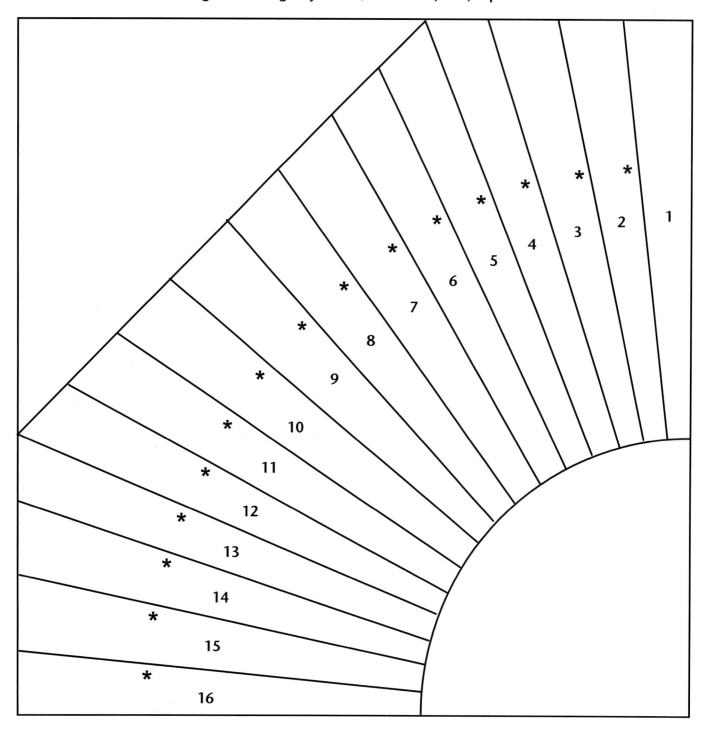

COUNTRY CONCERTO
plan 2

enlarge this design by 136%, to 25cm (10in) square

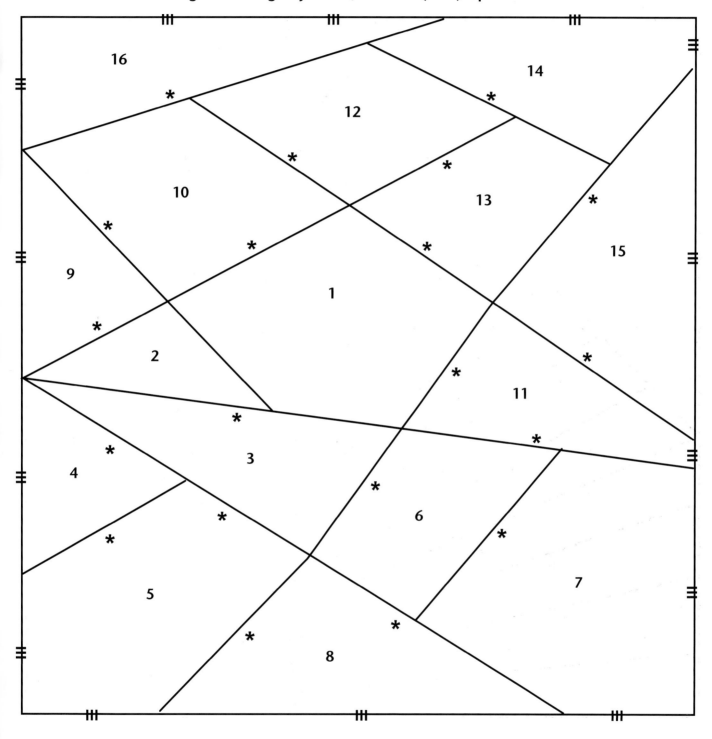

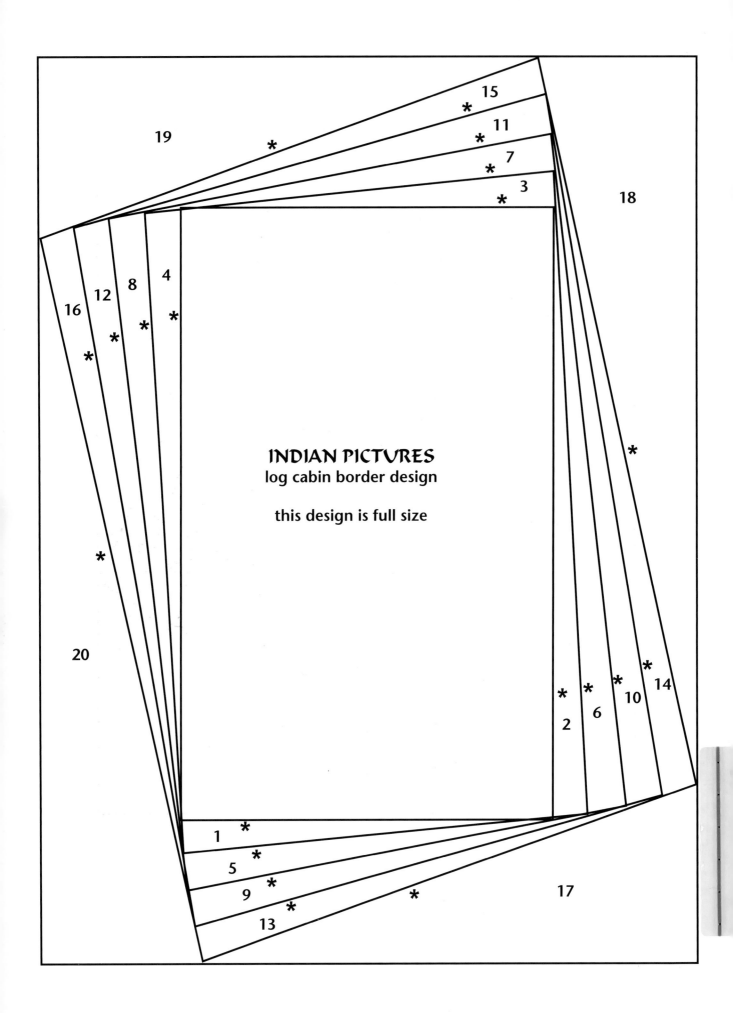

INDIAN PICTURES
log cabin border design

this design is full size

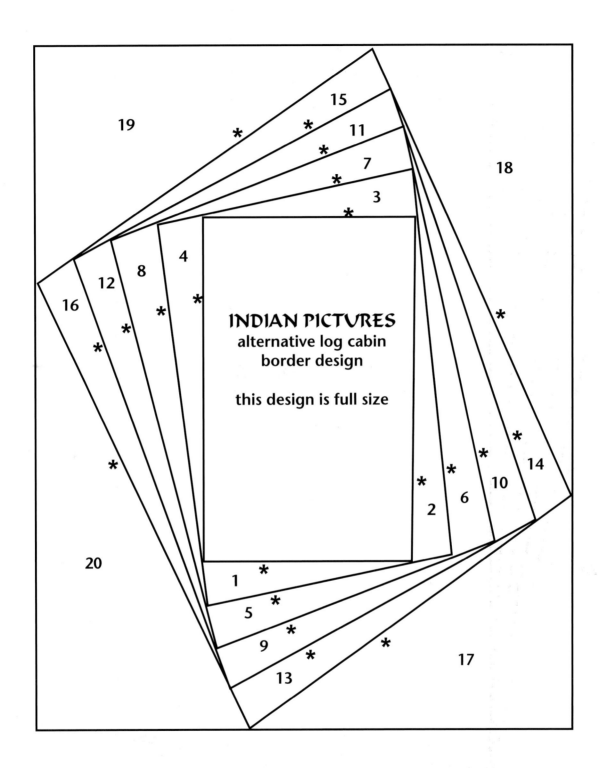

INDIAN PICTURES
alternative log cabin
border design

this design is full size

INDIAN PICTURES
embroidery designs

these designs
are full size

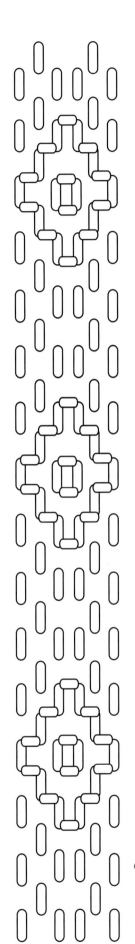

INDIAN PICTURES
embroidery design

INDIAN PICTURES
design for beaded border

these designs
are full size

117

• ACKNOWLEDGEMENTS

I want to thank the following people:

- Gail and Christopher Lawther, whose advice, support and professional skills ensured that this book was written and then published.

- Emma and Roger Cooling of Grosvenor Exhibitions Ltd, who have given me much support and encouragement.

- Traplet Publications, for accepting this book onto their list for 2003.

Particular thanks to Hilary Williams of The Silk Route for her generous advice and support over many years, and for her sponsorship.

Finally, thanks to my husband, for sharing the pains of authorship.

• PHOTO CREDITS

All photographs are by Gisela Thwaites except the following:

- Gisela in front of the Taj Mahal (page 4), taken by Dr Dick MacAuliffe

- photographs of fabrics from The Silk Route (page 12), taken by Hilary Williams

- photographs on pages 33, 35, 42, 48, 51, 53, 54, 64, 65, 70, 72, 75 and 79, taken by Teamwork

The photographs of *Kama* (see page 41) first appeared in *Sumptuous Patchwork* (editor Christine Donaldson), and are reproduced with the kind permission of Mrinalini Srivastava of Savitri Books.

The Indian Bird Rope pattern (see page 42) was first published in *Fabrications – Patchwork and Quilting with Embroidery*, February/March 2001 issue, and is reprinted with the kind permission of the editor, Emma Cooling.

• CONTACTING THE AUTHOR

If you'd like details of Gisela's talks, workshops and demonstrations, contact her at Rose Cottage, Rusper Road, Newdigate, Surrey RH5 5BX.

E-mail: donthwaites@onetel.net.uk

• FURTHER READING

Books on techniques and Indian textiles

Elegant Stitches Judith Baker Montano,
C&T Publishing 1995
ISBN 0-914881-85-X

Sumptuous Patchwork edited Christine Donaldson,
Ward Lock 1997
ISBN 0-7063-7615-5

The Techniques of Indian Embroidery Anne Morrell,
Batsford 1994
ISBN 0-7134-6410-0

Traditional Indian Textiles John Gillow and Nicholas Barnard, Thames and Hudson 1991
ISBN 0-5000-1491-4

Patolas and Resist-Dyed Fabrics of India
exhibition catalogue, Mapin Publishing Ltd
(Ahmedabad) 1998
ISBN 0-9441-4209-5

More general reading on India

Cultural Atlas of India Gordon Johnson,
Time Life Books 1995
ISBN 0-7054-0872-8
(a fascinating, highly-illustrated overview)

Rajasthan Francis Brunel,
UBSPD
ISBN 2-8551-8055-4
(a magnificently-illustrated portrait of the region)

An Indian Attachment Sarah Lloyd,
Eland 1992
ISBN 0-9078-7112-7
(an account of two years living in an Indian village)

Guidebooks

These are useful sources of ideas as well as being full of information on places and people. Ones I've found particularly helpful are:

India Companion Louise Nicholson, Headline 1996

India Handbook Footprint Series, latest edition

India Lonely Planet Series, latest edition

• SUPPLIERS IN THE UK

The Silk Route (mail order)
Cross Cottage
Cross Lane
Frimley Green
Surrey GU16 6LN
tel: 01252 835781
e-mail: hilary@thesilkroute.co.uk
website: www.thesilkroute.co.uk
textured silks, threads and fine silk ribbons

Stef Francis (mail order)
Waverley
High Rocombe
Stokeinteignhead
Newton Abbot
Devon TQ12 4QL
tel: 01803 323004
website: www.stef-francis.co.uk
space-dyed threads and fabrics, Indian 'crunches'

Out of Africa (mail order)
17 Bashford Way
Crawley
Sussex RH10 7FY
e-mail: outofafrica@tinyonline.co.uk
dyed batik and threads

Glitterati
Unit 1
Staples Corner Business Park
Suite 9, Big Yellow Offices
1000 North Circular Road
London NW2 7JP
tel: 020 7723 5556
*shisha (mirrors), braids, bindi, metallic threads,
brass bells and some beads*

Ells & Farrier
20 Beak Street
London NW2 7JP
tel: 020 7629 9964
a haven for beads

Liberty plc
Regent Street
London W1R 6AH
tel: 020 7573 9876
beautiful silk ribbons, braids and silk floss

The Quilt Room
20 West Street
Dorking
Surrey RH4 1BL
tel: 01306 877307
e-mail: sales@quiltroom.co.uk
website: www.quiltroom.co.uk
American muslin, fabrics, buttons and bells

Look out for these other titles in the